# CHICAGO EYEWITNESS

# CHICAGO EYEWITNESS

Mark Lane

Photographs by Carolyn Mugar

ASTOR-HONOR, INC. NEW YORK

As I left Chicago I could not erase the thoughts of bleeding heads, of coughing and vomiting youngsters, of the exhausted but tireless kids who could not be conquered by terror, or gas, or flailing clubs or guns. Do not weep for them, America. Your children, far braver than you, were a moment in the conscience of man.

# CONTENTS

# introduction

I found myself in Chicago toward the end of August, 1968. I went there neither because the Democratic Party convention was taking place at that time nor because there were to be street demonstrations. Before long I became a participant-observer in the street activities. I was almost always in the front line when the various "riots" erupted. With me was Carolyn Mugar, whose photographs appear in this work. I was present when each picture was taken.

This then, is a personal account of what I saw. I do not submit it as an objective and detached study of the events but as a report of what I, a quasi-demonstrator, experienced and saw. In a period of three days I was gassed four times and clubbed twice by the National Guard and the Chicago police although I had violated no law or ordinance. I was not seriously injured. Others

5

suffered far more, and this work is primarily about them. I mention my own encounters at this time merely to apprise the reader at the very outset of my involvement and possible bias. As I write these words, my chest and throat are raw with the toxic effects of tear gas.

Yet, at the outset, I do affirm as well that I honestly and carefully recorded the events as they transpired and that with the same degree of caution I have tried to present them accurately to you.

Was I a demonstrator or was I a reporter? I was neither, as I was both. I remained with the demonstrators for almost all of the time, using my press credentials to pass through police lines only when it seemed to me necessary to observe a particular event from another view. I had never seen a tank, or armed personnel carrier, in the streets of an American city before and I was anxious to have it photographed. As it was well beyond police lines one afternoon, only my press credentials permitted me access to it. I agreed with myself that I would not use those credentials to escape from a difficult situation no matter how serious the encounter became. On one occasion, through fear, I surrendered that principle, in the interest of self-protection. While most of the young people spent the early mornings resting or sleeping in the park, I retreated to a motel well outside of the zone of conflict at about three or four in the morning for a shower and a few hours sleep.

## INTRODUCTION

In a sense I was a war correspondent. I shared most of the dangers, and some, but by no means most, of the inconveniences. Read this account as you would read Ernie Pyle during World War II. Few feats of individual heroism by enemy soldiers found their way into his re-markable reports. He was in no position to observe them, nor probably would he have been inclined to relate them in any event. I was with the young people, not with the police and soldiers. I report what I saw.

CHAPTER I

# prologue

The French Quarter, as it is called by the tourists,
or the Quarter, as it is known to the residents, provides
a very pleasant environment for a writer so long as you
do not attempt to live on the Street, or Bourbon Street,
as you might know it. I live on Charles Street, a block
or two from the great Mississippi River, which I visit
daily and nightly. On the way there, I pass Jackson
Square with its lovely fountain commemorating the visit
of Charles de Gaulle to New Orleans just eight years ago;
the St. Louis Cathedral, America's oldest church; and the
park surrounded by portrait painters who are themselves
surrounded by leisurely strolling tourists. I walk through
the park with its flowering trees, bordered by the great
flat green leaves of the banana plants and breathe deep
the unique perfume of the vegetation as it combines with
the strange and not disagreeable smell of hops driven
into the park as the river breeze sweeps past the Jax

Brewery on the river's edge. Warm, unconflicted, unchallenging and pleasant. This has been part of my life for many months as my day-time, week-day hours have been devoted to exploring the district attorney's investigation into the death of President Kennedy.

This is the Quarter—an urban pastoral scene. A sazerac in the late afternoon at Arnaud's or the Napoleon House, dinner at Antoine's or the Vieux Carré. And always the great river at the door, rushing down from the north into the Gulf of Mexico as it did a thousand years ago; as it did when Mark Twain wrote about it. The sazeracs retain that New Orleans absinthe flavor, as they did when A. J. Liebling wrote *The Earl of Louisiana* All remains the same, for the river is the heart of the country and it is constant. It is now polluted, but one adjusts to pollution very quickly.

My new book has just been published and I am called upon to travel about the country and discuss it on radio and television programs. I almost resent the intrusion upon my new relaxed life. My last trip in connection with *A Citizen's Dissent* is planned for St. Petersburg, Florida, in just a few days. My telephone rings and a young lady from Philadelphia is offering me the Vice-Presidential nomination. I respond that my present work is too important to give up for that office, although I do not denigrate the important work that a Vice-President can do; that in my view I can best serve my fellow

10

citizens as their President; but that if the Presidential candidate, once selected, should call upon me to serve with him, I could not, in fairness to my obligation to assist my country, particularly during these trying days, turn him down. She responds, without a trace of humor, that she is serious. Oh, I ask, Vice-President of what?

She explains, patiently and very clearly, as if she might be talking to a child, that her organization has secured a place on the ballot in Pennsylvania for Dick Gregory for President. Mr. Gregory, she adds, asked them to ask me if I would run with him. Running for Vice-President of Pennsylvania, I muse to myself. Greg has been a good friend for some years and I agreed.

Two days later, Greg called. He asked if I would agree to be his running-mate in some other states where his name might also appear on the ballot and if I would join him as a national write-in candidate. I agreed and asked if I could fly to Chicago so that we might put our platform together and hold a press conference announcing our candidacy. I was about to agree when I thought of my St. Petersburg obligations. I can't make it until Tuesday night, I explained, and he said fine, he'd call the conference for Wednesday morning. He added that he would get a hotel room for me in advance. They will be hard to come by, he said, since the Democratic convention is just about to take place.

He told me that Chicago was in the midst of a taxi-cab drivers' strike and at the early stages of a bus drivers' strike and that he would arrange for a friend, Mike Watley, to meet me at the airport. Watley had been the director of the sky caps at the San Francisco airport. He gave up that rather lucrative assignment to drive Gregory around San Francisco when he performed at the Hungry I there and lectured at west coast colleges. Later when Gregory returned to Chicago, Watley joined him in order to perform the same services there. Watley is one of several living witnesses to Dick Gregory's odd charisma.

"You'll know him," Gregory said. "He's not a little fellow and he wears coveralls."

Tuesday, I flew from Florida to Chicago.

# CHAPTER II

# tuesday

Greg had engaged in understatement. Watley was huge. Although cleanly shaven, he wore the same type of clothing Gregory was committed to. Many months before, Greg had said that he would neither shave nor purchase new clothes until the war in Viet Nam ended. With a professionalism that betrayed his former occupation, Watley grabbed my suitcase and soon we were driving into town. From lamp posts, overpasses and pillars, signs with but one message greeted us: "Welcome to Chicago." Over Mayor Richard Daley's signature, "all delegates and visitors" were entreated to feel comfortable and at home."Yeah, welcome, all right," Watley mumbled half to himself as he pointed to the newspapers alongside us in the seat.

The Chicago dailies spoke of the "bloody confrontations" between the police and demonstrators the night before. Scores of young people had been beaten, hundreds gassed and many arrested as the police, according to the reports, had charged into Lincoln Park to enforce the eleven o'clock curfew.

Thousands of young people from various parts of the country had come to Chicago during the Democratic convention to demonstrate against the war. The exact number will perhaps never be established with any degree of certainty, but in police and newspaper estimates the approximate figure appearing most regularly was ten thousand.

Those referred to as the "leaders" of the protesters rarely offered an estimate and probably were less qualified to do so and in possession of less relevant information than the city officials and the newspaper employees. For the demonstration had no real leaders. To a very large extent, it just evolved.

Almost all of the demonstrators were in their late teens or early twenties. Few could afford hotel rooms and even fewer could have found an empty room had they sought one. Accordingly, many brought packs with sleeping bags or blankets and planned to sleep outside during that late August week. The weather was pleasant and they expected that many of their friends would be there.

Technically, the law requires that the parks be va-

14

cated by eleven, but that law has been honored histor-
ically more by its breach than by its execution. One newspaper columnist was asked to write a special column
welcoming visiting newsmen and delegates to Chicago.
In the *Chicago Daily News* he wrote, "Don't hesitate to
walk on the grass or to spread your coat and take a nap.
Chicago likes its parks to be used by people so you won't

"Chicago likes its parks to be used by people . . ." The
National Guard encamped behind barbed wire in the
center of Chicago.

see any 'Keep Off the Grass' signs. And you can feel safe in the park. It is well-patrolled by policemen, and many Chicagoans sleep there on hot nights."

David Dellinger, active with one of the sponsoring groups, had sought to arrange for a meeting with the city administration so that permission to sleep in some park might be secured, but the Mayor's office declined to meet with him. In the interim, the Lincoln Park Citizens Committee, comprised of clergymen and prominent laymen in the Lincoln Park area, called upon the police to lift the ban against sleeping in Lincoln Park.

The Rev. Raymond A. Schroth, a Jesuit who resides at Georgetown University and teaches at George Washington University, spoke of brutality that he had witnessed on Monday afternoon in Grant Park. Then he said that the Poor People's Campaign in Washington "was supposed to be illegal on government land, but the government, through Attorney-General Ramsey Clark, accomodated it." Father Schroth added, "Young people are coming to Chicago to be part of what's happening. They want a good stab at taking part in the democratic process before it goes. Really the arrival of these dissenters is an act of hope. They didn't go to Miami (the Republican convention) because there was no hope in being present in that situation for them."

Mayor Daley was adamant and on Monday night and

16

early Tuesday morning the police entered the park. The *Chicago Sun-Times* reported that "scores of persons suffered injuries inflicted by club swinging police." Tear gas was employed as well. The Lincoln Park Citizens Emergency Committee said that the police, not the demonstrators, constituted "a clear and imminent danger to the community." The Committee added that citizens of the community were "indiscriminately gassed and beaten on our neighborhood streets."

After the events of Monday evening, a Commission of the Presbytery of Chicago issued a public statement deploring "unwarranted police brutality." The Presbytery warned that "if these vicious tactics are continued, they could cause complete lack of faith in the police department and create a major city-wide conflict."

Press service stories speaking candidly of police excesses were given front page placement by newspapers throughout the country. For example, *United Press International* reported that youngsters in the park were removed by "police who sprayed them with tear gas and descended on them with clubs." For once the press made no references to "allegations" or "charges" of brutality by law-enforcement officers; the allegations and charges were made by the newspaper reporters, and read as fact by millions of Americans. Perhaps at least part of the reason for the new approach by the press was caused by a new approach by the police.

17

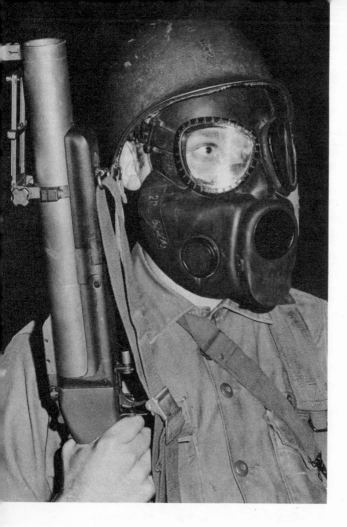

A soldier in a gas mask.

It soon became apparent that the police had agreed to give special treatment to reporters and photographers.

Those carrying cameras and those with press credentials obviously displayed were often sought out by police officers and beaten. The *Washington Post* noted that, "The Chicago technique for keeping photographers of police brutality from public view is a very simple one: it is to club photographers, smash cameras and confiscate film."

Jack Mabley, the leading columnist for *Chicago's American,* and until convention week the police department's strongest supporter, wrote that he witnessed the senseless beating of a crippled bystander by police officers. He also said that he, himself, had been menaced by a policeman in a gas mask who "leveled his rifle at me." He wrote that he saw the unprovoked clubbing of one of his colleagues: "A policeman clubbed him to the ground as he shouted his identity and waved his press card." The reporter, Mabley said, "was not interfering with police work. He had been standing on the sidewalk talking with a plainclothesman he knew." Mabley added that some reporters who had been beaten "were singled out and deliberately chased down because they had cameras." Mabley had stoutly defended the tight security in a page-one story on the eve of the convention as he wrote of the threats to law and order posed by the "hippies" and "dangerous revolutionaries." However, before the convention had ended he wrote, "This is not the beginning of the police state, it is the police state."

Jim Hampton, writing in the *National Observer* noted

that "the hours of close contact, and the beatings administered to some thirty newsmen by Chicago police, forged a foxhole camaraderie between some newsmen and some protesters." He added that "camaraderie, as it will, bred understanding."

Reporters tend, in most instances, to report an establishment view. There are exceptions, of course, but on occasion the exceptional story, although written, is not published in any event. I have tried cases as a defense lawyer for some seventeen years and I have personal knowledge of the cynical reaction of the press to claims, and even proof, of inordinate violence instigated by law officers. Something unique was occuring in the streets of Chicago, however, and not only there. Even on the floor of the convention, reporters were experiencing discomfort while other reporters looked on.

Dan Rather, a *CBS-TV* reporter, was among the first of the casualties within the convention hall. He reported, "A security man just slugged me in the stomach." Walter Cronkite, the network's ordinarily cool anchor man, his voice quivering with anger, said, "These are a bunch of thugs we are seeing here." In the streets it was much worse. *Newsweek's* news editor, Hal Bruno, made the assignments for that publication's staff and he prescribed the tactics as well: "Travel in pairs and wear riot helmets at all times." When the week ended, despite the precautions, *Newsweek* reported six casualties of its street staff of nine. A bureau chief "clubbed on the ribs;" a photographer "beaten on back and legs;" three reporters "clubbed on leg," "jabbed in stomach" and "beaten on back and leg" respectively; a trainee "clubbed on back." The magazine commented that all the injured were "wearing prominent press credentials." A reporter for that publication said that he heard a policeman order, "Get the cameras and beat the press."

Paul Sequeira, a photographer for the *Chicago Daily News*, was attacked twice while working. He reported that a police lieutenant fired Chemical Mace at him, but he ducked out of the way. Later he took a picture of an off-duty soldier beating a demonstrator. A number of policemen moved in on him. "I held out my press card and hollered, "Press,' at them," he said, "but they started swinging." Sequeira's right hand was broken.

A photographer for *Washington Post*, Steven Nothrup, was also attacked twice in one evening. He was knocked off his feet when he tried to take pictures of police chasing a group of demonstrators. Later, when he observed police chasing a girl into a hedge and beating her, he tried to photograph the scene. He was beaten with a nightstick.

*Time* reported that John Linstead of the *Chicago Daily News* "was covering the street demonstration during the Democratic convention when he spotted Chicago policemen clubbing three girls Linstead believed to be

21

bystanders. 'For God's sake, stop that,' Linstead shouted at the police. For his troubles, he was cracked on the head and wound up in the hospital for two days." The event is less startling, in the contemporary American context, than is the factual reporting of it in *Time*.

Two important questions present themselves for consideration, for they represent a distinct departure from the past:

Why did the police attack the reporters? Why did the press report the extent of the police brutality accurately?

The police hoped that by confiscating film and destroying cameras, no photographic record of their attacks upon the demonstrators would exist. *Chicago's American* stated editorially that it was "clear that, in most cases, the club-swingers zeroed in on photographers who had taken pictures that might prove embarrassing to the police." Beating newsmen on the scene probably was calculated to diminish press coverage, thereby leaving the police free to deal with the young demonstrators in relative seclusion. *Newsweek* suggested that "more significant, many policemen felt a deep resentment for the press that was reinforced by Mayor Daley's conspicious contempt for newsmen." Surely the degree of energy and commitment, not to say enthusiasm, that the police brought to their task appeared to disclose a deep resentment and a knowledge that punishment from Mayor Daley's office would not be forthcoming.

The public-information officer for the Chicago police said at a press conference, "This unruly group of revolutionaries is bent on the destruction of our system of government. They represent a pitiful handful." And then he added ("bitterly" accordingly to *Newsweek*), "But by golly, they get the cooperation of the news media." As official Chicago saw it, the newsmen were important partners in the demonstration, without whose encouragement the protesters would not have come to the city.

Why did the police attack the reporters? Probably for three reasons. They wanted to be able to assault the demonstrators without fear of coverage. They viewed the reporters with hostility. They were aware that the city administration, if not encouraged the assaults, would at least nod in silent approval.

Why did the press report the facts?

*Newsweek* recognized that an important change had taken place. "Traditionally," the magazine wrote, "of course, the press by and large has known where it stood. Until very recently, reporters have run with the hounds rather than held with the hares."

In the past many of the victims of police excesses have been Negroes, Mexican Americans, Puerto Ricans

23

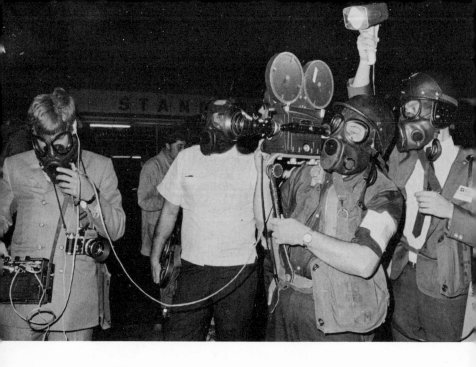

An NBC-TV crew about to conduct a street interview.
No longer "running with the hounds".

or other ghetto dwellers. While it was difficult for the
reporters and their employers to identify with that body
of deprived America, little imagination was required to
understand the plight of a beaten newsman, particularly
if you were the newsman who had been struck. Empathy,
like charity, begins at home. For example, Cronkite's
detachment, very much in evidence as boys and girls

24

were illegally assaulted in the streets, some sustaining serious head injuries and broken bones, deserted him when one almost superficial blow was dealt to a colleague.

Some of the young demonstrators with whom I spoke suspected that the reporters permitted their new-found hostility to police brutality to constrain them to report the facts, more because police batons had been aimed at some press representatives than due to the savage attacks upon the protesters and the denial of their constitutional guarantees. Yet this is perhaps oversimplification.

It was also possible for the reporters to identify with the young people for another reason. They were primarily white and from middle class, "respectable" homes. They were, in fact, the kind of clients a lawyer knows he may make a successful pitch for when pleading for parole rather than bail. It may have been difficult for some reporters to understand what the protesters were about, and the generation gap may have made the methods of the young totally inexplicable to the middle-aged but identification with the youngsters was easy. They were children that the reporters had raised.

Tom Wicker, whose sense of outrage is rarely engaged, wrote in the *New York Times* that the demonstrators were mostly "idealistic, demonstrably brave, concerned about their country and their fellow men." He concluded,

"The truth is that these were our children in the streets and the Chicago police beat them up."

Blacks and the poor are sometimes brave and concerned as well, but as the Kerner Commission noted, the only time the reporters for the major daily newspapers visit the ghetto areas is behind police skirmish lines during riots. Some of the relatively few Negroes in the demonstration appeared to be aware of the reason for the new press objectivity. In fact a Negro reporter for the *Chicago Defender* said to some white news reporters after the convention had left Chicago, "I'm really glad you people got your asses busted. Now you know what happens in the ghetto every night."

Yet in spite of the suspicions of the young as to the selfish origins of the new objectivity and regardless of the bitter-sweet reaction of the blacks who were now sharing their burden with the white man, a new day for journalism had dawned. "They" had become "we." And as a result, despite powerful reasons for not doing so, the press reported the facts. Soon, too soon, the media were to retreat in panic, but for the moment the American people had immediate access to the pertinent information.

As I rode toward the one integrated section of the city where Dick Gregory lived with his family, I read with incredulity the police attacks upon the press. As I read the reports, Police Superintendent James B. Conlisk Jr. met with a seventeen man delegation of media representatives. A flood of protests from three of Chicago's daily newspapers, all three networks and various journalistic, religious and civic organizations had been directed to Daley and to Conlisk. Four aldermen had called for an official censure of Daley, and the Chicago Newspaper Guild stated that if Conlisk "cannot control his men he should resign."

Gregory was at home waiting for me. I said, "Well I guess I missed all the excitement." He answered, "Just hang around town, there's more to come." I told him that the establishment had cracked down on Daley, that just about all of the media supported by many important and powerful organizations had demanded an end to the attacks. He said, "Hell man, they don't mean a thing. This whole thing is programmed. The attacks will get worse not better. The Chicago cops aren't so bad. You should see how nice they are when the Shriners come to town. They help the drunk ones back to their hotels. Why, they don't even complain if they throw mattresses out of their windows. It's not the cops. They are coming on like America's new niggers. The fault starts at the top. They are following orders. And those orders are not about to change. Man, Chicago is a police state."

I said that a single unprovoked attack, or even a number of unprovoked attacks, by the police did not make a police state. I suggested that it was necessary

27

for the society to have time to react to police excesses before the full measure of the society could be taken. "What the police do now, after the widespread revulsion with their actions has been registered, will determine what we have become," I said. The dictionary definition of police state—"A nation in which police suppress any act by an individual or group that conflicts with governmental policy or principle"—I argued, was at the same time too broad and too narrow. "*Any act*," I said, "was too broad a gauge, so at times any society could be vulnerable to the charge." Had a dozen SS members killed a number of Jews in Berlin one day, we would not, on that evidence alone, be justified in calling Germany a police state. Transgressions, however brutal, however lamentable, cannot be proof that the nature of society has been altered. If such actions are commended by the leadership as required and necessary and proper, as was the case in Hitler's Germany, then the appellation is valid. To condone is to accept the past, and to accept as well, responsibility for similar actions in the future.

That evening we visited Lincoln Park, where Gregory was to speak. The scene was peaceful, almost pastoral, as youngsters nestled on the grass. Tiny bonfires made of single sheets of newspaper dotted the area, and no doubt inspired the singing of *The Battle Hymn of the Republic*. It was not yet curfew time.

We left to appear at the Lyndon Johnson Unbirthday

Party at the Chicago Coliseum. Before we arrived, Jean Genet, William Burroughs and Allen Ginsberg had spoken. Genet said that the audience, consisting of about three thousand, and comprising the first and only regular meeting of those in Chicago, had responded to the Democratic "clownish convention, which indeed is conventional, by your demonstrations in the park, which are filled with poetry." Ginsberg said, "We wanted to sleep in the park, not confront hired historical phantoms armed with tear gas, revolvers, acting definite roles written for them by egoists in City Hall." Paul Krassner was speaking as we arrived, combining bad taste with insight, unfortunately in unequal measure. Hubert Humphrey, he said, had already selected his Vice-Presidential running-mate. "The man he's selected is the man who is responsible for Hubert Humphrey's success, and they've already printed posters with his arm around Sirhan Sirhan."

The audience responded well to Krassner, and it is worthwhile to consider why that is so. The response was not to witticisms offered, in spite of their poor taste, but the applause and laughter seemed to flow from the exposure of the vulgarity. I am perhaps too old to appreciate the humor, but interested enough to try to understand its basis. The young people rarely employed profanity in ordinary conversation with each other. I use it far more frequently myself. Yet later that night, I confess to experiencing embarrassment as two thousand youngsters gathered outside the Conrad Hilton Hotel, at which many of the delegates had registered, chanted a rather odd birthday greeting to their anti-hero—"Fuck you, Lyndon Johnson."

Ask them about their clothes and they speak of their refusal to wear "middle class costumes." If you are in the mainstream of American life, and if you wish to understand the young, begin with the knowledge that they do not wish to understand you. For you, middle-class America, are not even the enemy. No such dignity has been conferred upon you. You are merely irrelevant. Their public pronouncements of profanity, rare though they are, have nothing to do with them. It is just one manifestation of middle-class value rejection. A positive reaction to Krassner is another. Differences, some almost contrived—differences in clothing, hair style, speech—are all offered as proof of alienation from a thoroughly unsatisfactory society.

The press called the protestors "hippies," or the recently manufactured term, signifying nothing, "yippies." The terms are inaccurately applied. I recall being visited by a Danish journalist, Per Hanghoj, while I was living at Stanford University during the days when Haight-Ashbury, the hippy concentration community, was thriving in San Francisco. He was anxious to make a study of the phenomenon and we drove into town. Hanghoj asked at a book store, now referred to as a head shop, if there

30

was some bar where the hippies assembled, as he wished to interview them. The owner replied in a somewhat offended tone, "Hippies don't drink." Hanghoj said quickly, "Surely they eat. Is there some restaurant where I might find some?" They do eat but they do not protest. And they do not demonstrate. The classic hippy is dedicated to resolution of inner conflict and to seeking a beautiful existence or, at least, experience. Wicker of the *New York Times* was correct. Most of the demonstrators were concerned about their country and their fellow men. The press, then, was wrong. These were not the hippies of the middle sixties, they were the emerging activists of the seventies. A new youth had been born, a new generation had come forward, promising to be far better than we had ever known before. And no one had noticed.

Dick Gregory was the closing speaker. "Premier Kosygin just sent a cablegram to Mayor Richard J. Daley and asked him to send him 2,000 Chicago cops. There's no doubt they could settle things in Czechoslovakia in about fifteen minutes. There's got to be something insane about a system that keeps calling for law and order when the poor want to stand up for their rights, but that lets almost every major city remain controlled by the crime syndicate. What you have decided to do about the system is something that we old fools should have started doing a long time ago. The price for what you are trying to do is worth getting knocked for and stomped

31

on for. I hope you don't let them turn you around, and I hope that the more tear gas they pour on you, the more determined you will become to break this damn system." The *National Observer* reported that at that moment "the hall exploded with cheering." Gregory closed with the observation that if our form of society "is as good as we claim it is, why the hell do we have to go ramming it down people's throats with guns?"

We remained at the Coliseum for some time talking to members of the audience and then drove toward the Conrad Hilton and Grant Park directly across the street from the hotel. The police filled Michigan Avenue, and bus load after bus load of police reinforcements arrived. Just after 1:30 a police official announced that no effort would be made that night to remove the demonstrators from Grant Park if they remained peaceful. The crowd cheered. Stragglers came from Lincoln Park reporting that they had been gassed and beaten there. At 3:00 the National Guard relieved the police while delegates and alternates to the convention addressed the protesters to endorse their cause. The behavior of the demonstrators had been consistent both nights. Yet on Monday there had been widespread gassing and many severe injuries inflicted, while this Tuesday night, or Wednesday morning, there was neither at Grant Park. It became quite clear who was responsible for the rioting—the demonstrators or the police.

32

I picked up some newspapers and read them on the way home—home being a small motel room located in the black South Side. The *Chicago Sun-Times* gave the most detailed account of the meeting with Conlisk, perhaps because Emmett Dedmon, editor of that newspaper, was also spokesman for the media executives. The police had agreed to enforce the Department regulation which calls for suspension of officers who remove badges or name tags. Before attacking the newsmen, many police officers had had the presence of mind to remove both. The Department agreed to make an "immediate police investigation of the unprovoked attack on a *Newsweek* reporter Monday night." Evidently no such agreement was reached regarding the other fifteen reporters and photographers who had been injured to the point where medical attention was required. It was also announced that there was "an agreement that policemen would not confiscate or otherwise take communications equipment from newsmen, including tape recorders, cameras and film."

The final concession in the four-point agreement was the "immediate ordering of a special police unit, including officers of at least lieutenant rank, to be stationed at sites of possible disturbances for the balance of the week. The unit's role will be to assure protection of the rights of the press and of bystanders." A cynic might observe that the request which brought about the fourth concession might be analogous to Custer calling for more Indians. Yet it was no less startling than the police agreement to refrain, in the future, from stealing from the newsmen; and no odder than the Department's concession to enforce its own rules regarding officer identification. Dedmon reported that the editors and other representatives were satisfied with the steps, and Conlisk "immediately issued an order implementing the agreement."

It is now not much before dawn. Gregory and I agreed to meet in a few hours for a press conference at a downtown hotel. While I slept, the young people kept vigil in the park.

# CHAPTER III

# wednesday a.m.

I walked past the Conrad Hilton. Masses of armed National Guardsmen were still there, guarding the eighty demonstrators who were left. Some youngsters sat on the grass in the park while others stretched and walked about. A few remained curled up in sleeping bags. The press commented upon the disheveled look of the young people. As was the case with the reporters, I came upon the scene fresh from a shower, a shave and a change of clothing. The youngsters in the park were denied such luxuries. I marvelled that they looked so fresh under the circumstances. I remembered too well being on bivouac for a couple of weeks during the war. Perhaps I should identify it as World War II, there having been a couple since. I was eighteen at the time, about the age of many in the park last night. At the end of one week, I was far less presentable than the long haired, oddly attired park tenants. About the clothing — a suit, white shirt and dark tie would hardly be serviceable for camping out. Many disdained such apparel for reasons of principle, as we have already stated. Others, who do dress in that fashion on occasion, put on more practical garb, designed to weather a week in the open air. But whatever the reason, their clothing, hair style and lack of general neatness tended to alienate many citizens from them and caused some of them to appear as special targets for police rage. This reaction to the superficial served only to reinforce the youngsters' judgment that much was amiss and much required change. And thus the cycle went, alienation causing further alienation, until it became plain that parents and children had precious little in common.

There, of course, were exceptions. Joe Garogiola of the *Today Show* commented upon what he had witnessed the night before. I never had considered the former St. Louis catcher to be particularly sensitive to the feelings of the "way out kids" as he described them. I was surprised to hear him relate his exchange with one of the youngsters. The boy had told Garogiola that he was afraid to go back into the streets, that he feared the night sticks and the gas. When asked why he was going, the lad replied that he had to. Suddenly the interviewer's prejudice against the clothing and the long hair vanished, the meaningless differences became immaterial. Garogiola said that he would have been proud if his own child had acted that way. "I taught them to do what they think is right, regardless of what others think and regardless of the cost," he said. Thus for such diverse personalities as Wicker of the *Times* and Garogiola of the Cardinals, the demonstrators were not a mass of hippies but dedicated individuals. To many others, particularly those of authoritarian tendencies, they were a threatening mob, devoted to tearing down the society. While many of the youngsters would have preferred the more romantic latter description, it was nonetheless inaccurate. They came to support the basic institutions, not to destroy them, as I was soon to learn when I shared the tear gas, the rifle butts, the police clubs and the all pervasive fear and panic with them.

It was time for the press conference, and I hurried along after discovering that many of the young people had gone to other more secluded parks with the dawn, while still others slept on floors in friends' apartments or in churches. The conference was well attended. Dick Gregory announced that we were running for President and Vice-President, that we would appear on the ballot in a number of states, including New York and Pennsylvania, and that we would be write-in candidates in all other states.

*Q.* What would you do if you met George Wallace while campaigning?

*Gregory.* Well, after we shook hands, thank him.

37

*Q.* Why thank him?

*Gregory.* He is performing a service. White liberals have always said that there are just a few bigots in the country, mostly in the South. Wallace will make it possible for us to ascertain the full extent of bigotry in America. When that vote is counted, a lot of things are going to change. Your Negro moderates are going to become black nationals The black nationals are going to become active radicals. What the active radicals are going to become I just don't know. You better think about it though.

*Q.* Mr. Lane, do you think you have a chance of actually winning?

*Lane.* Well, I am on a political winning streak. I ran for public office once, for the New York State Assembly, and I was elected.

*Q.* Do you think you may actually be elected?

*Lane.* Of course not. But our running provides a choice for those who wish to vote against the war. We are making it possible for them to vote on election day and still be able to face their children over the dinner table that night.

*Q.* How do you answer the charge by liberals that you may actually help to elect Nixon by taking votes away from Humphrey?

Dick Gregory announced that we were running for President and Vice-President.

*Lane.* I cannot be frightened by the spectre of Nixon, for we have lived with the reality of Johnson and Humphrey too long. No doubt, discerning liberals could detect a distinction between candidates if Hermann Wilhelm Goering were to run against Joseph Paul Goebbels. It is true that no two men are exactly alike, and from that truism we may take some solace as we consider the last years under Johnson. Yet their policies may be insufficiently dissimilar to cause decent men to be repulsed.

*Q.* Mr. Gregory, do you think you can be elected on a write-in?

*Gregory.* Lincoln was elected as a write-in candidate.

*Q.* How do you stand on the question of law and order?

*Gregory.* You know I'm running for President, not sheriff, like the other two candidates. Daley stands for law and order too. But his city is controlled by the crime syndicate.

*Q.* How do you approach that issue, Mr. Lane?

*Lane.* I believe in justice. Law is theoretically designed as a means toward justice. Order results when it, the law, does provide justice. The goal has to be justice. Law and order will follow. Conversely, without justice there will be no tranquility, no peace in this country. And there shouldn't be.

*Q.* Thank you, gentlemen.

Greg and I agreed to meet the next morning on our platform. I had a free afternoon in Chicago. After a very late and leisurely lunch, I thought of calling a friend or two at *Playboy Magazine.*

Instead I met Carolyn Mugar, a photographer from Cambridge, Massachusetts, and we strolled over toward the Conrad Hilton. I do not suppose that I will ever forget the next forty-eight hours.

40

CHAPTER IV

# wednesday afternoon in grant park

The Hilton area was deserted except for the police. An outdoor meeting was taking place at Grant Park east of the Illinois Central tracks and beyond Columbus Drive. The police surrounded the meeting. The *Chicago Daily News* reported that "police tempers were already frayed by a youth who burned a draft delinquency notice at the rally." For the police that day, and for the entire week, viewed themselves as instruments of justice and of punishment, not as peace officers. Suddenly a big bearded man, known as Bob (Big Man) Lavin, charged toward an American flag in the park. The *Chicago Daily News* said, "A fight broke out as they (the police) attempted to arrest a hippie who hauled the American flag at half staff. As the police moved in, two tear gas cannisters exploded, fights broke out and policemen swung their clubs. Among the first victims was Rennie Davis, who served as a director of the organization sponsoring the rally."

Later, Mayor Daley was to issue a 77 page report in support of the police. Of this incident, the report said, a "young male," not identified by name, "began to lower the American flag from the main flag pole. His companions were arranging a black flag of anarchy for substitution when a squad of eight to ten police rushed the base of the pole and arrested the individual." The Mayor's report stated that the crowd reacted by throwing objects and that "a squad of about 40 police rushed through the crowd swinging their night sticks."

Both the press and the Mayor's report were substantially correct in stating that the riot erupted as a result of the police reaction to the attempt to lower the flag. Yet there was no need for imprecision on the part of the Mayor's report in identifying the person responsible for the flag lowering. His name is Robert L. Pierson. He employed the alias Bob (Big Man) Lavin and affected a beard as a disguise. He is a police officer. In a front page, copyrighted story, the *Chicago Tribune* published an exclusive interview with him on Saturday, August 31. On Wednesday, when he served as a police agent provocateur, his police connections were unknown to the young people assembled in Grant Park, who tried to assist him when he appeared to be attacked. When Mayor Daley's report was issued, Pierson's police background was public knowledge. Yet Daley's report makes no mention of the fact that the proximate cause of the riot in Grant Park

42

and the serious injuries sustained by many youthful demonstrators, was one of Mayor Daley's own employees. The *Chicago Tribune* was able to secure an exclusive interview with Pierson, no doubt due to the fact that it had maintained good relations with the Police Department throughout the difficult week. This was possible for the *Tribune* even though its own reporters were threatened with beatings by the police without provocation. For example, the *Chicago Tribune* reported, "A *Tribune* reporter who was at the melee in Lincoln Park early yesterday reported that police told him that he would get his 'head busted' if he continued to stay near the demonstration." Two days later, in a front page editorial, that newspaper wrote, "For enforcing law and order, Mayor Daley and the police deserve congratulations rather than criticism." It referred to Chicago as "this orderly city" and stated that the *Tribune* was proud of Chicago's "lovely parks." While such an uncritical view of the events could hardly be calculated to inspire confidence in one's employees, it evidently had the desired effect with the police department.

In the interview Pierson told the *Tribune* that he participated in the action which "lowered an American flag in Grant Park" and which "touched off rioting as police moved in." The Daley report states with some degree of exaggeration, but not without some basis, that the police were "showered with bottles, sticks, rocks and other objects." The word "shower" conjures up an image of a rain of debris. In the days that I observed the confrontations, I did see a number of objects hurled toward police lines. I saw a few empty plastic containers that had previously been discarded by the medical corps fly into the police lines. The crazy path they described while flying through the air revealed them to be without much substance. They were light in weight and could hardly do any real damage to the helmeted officers. They were thrown in each instance by a person or persons far behind the front lines and I never could see who was responsible. I do not doubt that more substantial objects were thrown as well, on rare occasion. The source of this information is police officer Pierson. He told the *Tribune* that he "was clubbed by police" on three separate occasions and added that the clubbings were "not without provocation." In addition he revealed that he "threw rocks and bottles and hurled insults at police" on Monday night. He said that Tuesday night he "threw more bottles." On Wednesday afternoon, Pierson played a role in starting the riot in Grant Park; but then, fearing that he was recognized, he abandoned his undercover assignment for a safer one, he said.

To fully gauge the city's irresponsibility in employing police officers assigned to institute disorder on both sides of the line, one must do more than read the dry statistics of the number injured. When you see two burly police officers chase a young girl, drag her into the bushes by the hair, then club here until she is senseless, and leave her bleeding profusely from a head wound, all without provocation on her part, you have witnessed something that you cannot soon forget. As you watch the clubbing, you know that if you go to her aid you too will be clubbed and so you walk away; but you cannot avoid hearing the distinctive dull thud as you walk.

And so I decided to observe no more from the outside, but to join each demonstration. And to be in the front lines of each confrontation. I am a lawyer. I have been a lawmaker as well. I decided to violate no law, but to exercise fully my rights as a citizen.

# CHAPTER V

# late afternoon
# on the way to the amphitheatre

It is 4:30. A voice from a portable bull horn states that there will be a non-violent march to the Democratic convention some four and one half miles away. Most of the demonstrators drift away. About one thousand remain. We are in Grant Park, connected with the downtown area only by a series of bridges that cross the railroad tracks to our west. The leadership could not have chosen a more disadvantageous place to begin.

The police have been handing out leaflets all afternoon stating that no permit has been issued for a march and that all those who participate will be arrested.

A police car drives slowly past with an officer holding a bull horn. He advises the demonstrators they will be arrested if they try to march from there. I know I have a right to walk through the streets of Chicago and the local police do not have the right to reject an application for a permit. The proposed march is legal. Neither a police leaflet nor a police public address system can repeal a constitutional guarantee. I join the line of march.

It is five o'clock and we are formed in a long column of eight with arms linked together. On Columbus Drive,

I join the line of march . . . a long column of eight with arms linked together.

a large Hertz truck, rented by *ABC-TV*, passes very slowly. The crew members are all wearing blue helmets. A sign on the truck reads, "ABC News-Unconventional." We walk from the park toward Columbus Drive. Soldiers drive by in Army two-and-one-half-ton trucks just a few yards away. They are armed with M-1 rifles, and they wear gas masks. Two fully equipped United States Army helicopters circle above us. Curled barbed wire embankments are already established on the west side of Columbus Drive. Hundreds of police officers march past in formation. Each wears a pistol. Each carries a night stick. Each wears a light blue helmet. I look above the marchers as the police march past. All I can see is an ocean of light blue as the helmets bob and weave, moving north on Columbus. The demonstrators begin to chant, "More Pay for Cops. More Pay for Cops." Most in our line of march seem frightened. They do not expect to be arrested. They fully expect to be beaten and gassed. Some smear vaseline on their faces as a protection against skin burns caused by the gas. Many have little pieces of wet cloth to breathe through when the gas comes. I have none. A young, frail girl in the line of march tears her cloth in two and offers me half. I take it and thank her.

Perhaps twenty of the thousand wear helmets and most of them appear to be motorcyclists who decided to keep the head gear on for the march. With boring regularity, a mechanical voice drones from the head of the line,

"This is a non-violent march. Look, if non-violence is not your bag, please leave the line of march. The police have agents among us. If anyone starts to throw anything he probably is a cop." A few demonstrators correct the speaker. "A pig. Not a cop. A pig." The speaker, so non-violent he cannot accept that designation for a police agent, continues, "Well anyway, if anyone throws anything, he is not with us. Stop him. This is a non-violent march." I smiled at the assurance that there were police spies among us, thinking it a trifle heavy handed. Later, of course, I was to discover that it was an accurate assessment of the situation.

The demonstrators begin to sing — "Mine eyes have seen the glory of the coming of the Lord." Minutes later buses filled with police officers fill Columbus Drive. "More Pay for Cops." Do they chant from fear and in hopes of placating the officers, I wonder? Or do they see the police as underpaid workers with whom they can identify? A police car cruises past again: "This is not an authorized march. You are libel for arrest unless you leave this area now." No one leaves.

The head of the line has almost reached Balbo Drive. The march halts. Rows of police brandishing clubs have blocked the way. The police are three deep. Behind them, back some thirty yards are more than 300 soldiers. The soldiers prevent the marchers from going anywhere but back into the park. The loud-speaker informs us that

49

The march halts.

someone on our behalf will meet with the city officials to
see if we may be given permission to march. Until then we
are to wait. Some in the line sigh with exasperation, some
with relief. We wait. It is 5:30 and we still are waiting for some word.

I walk up to the head of the line, flank the police by
walking east and then circle back to study the soldiers.

The soldiers prevent the marchers from going anywhere but back into the park.

A wave of something akin to nostalgia sweeps over me for I have not seen those green fatigues, helmets with helmet liner, canteens, M-1 rifles with fixed but sheathed bayonets held in the ready position, for twenty years. I approach one soldier. He levels his rifle at me. I am surprised and certainly nostalgic no longer. "Listen, Sonny, didn't they teach you not to point that thing at anyone?" No answer. I continue, "I carried one of those things in

World War II, but I never expected to see the M-1 pointed at American citizens." No answer. I walk back to my position in line by flanking the police line again. The marchers are no longer in formation. Many are sitting on the grass, others milling about. Some begin to talk to officers who distribute circulars warning of arrest if the march proceeds. A demonstrator asks why he will be arrested. An officer answers, "You got no permit." The demonstrator answers, "We applied but you wouldn't issue a permit." "It's not up to me," the officer replies. A pretty, very young, very blonde girl explains to an officer whose eyes search her body — unprofessionally, that is, not as if he expects to find a weapon — "You see, many of us come from states without primaries. The only way we can vote, can hope to influence the delegates, is to be seen at the Amphitheatre. We don't want to hurt the delegates. We don't even want to see them. We just want to be close enough so that they can see us. Is that unreasonable?" No answer. "Why must we be kept miles away? Why can't we let the delegates know we're for McCarthy?" The officer shrugs and says, "He got no chance anyway," and walks away.

It is after 6:30. There is a conference at the head of the procession. The line forms again and we await word. Ten minutes pass. Some spectators begin to gather on the west side of Columbus Drive. The marchers signal peace and chant — "Join Us, Join Us." The peace sig-

The marchers signal peace and chant, "Join us. Join us."

nal? Two fingers raised in a "V" that once meant victory but now symolizes peace, or victory over, not through, war.

The sun is beginning to set. It is quite clear to all, except our leaders, that we will not be given permission to march. We begin to be concerned about being sealed off from the city as it gets dark. Finally, an announcement from the head of the line.

53

The leadership has capitulated. The announcement is, "We cannot proceed as a group without pushing into the officers; and since this is a non-violent demonstration, we cannot do that. The police have agreed that if we break up now we can go individually across the street to the area in front of the Hilton. So that's what we are going to do."

Most grumble their disagreement, but the decision has been made. The march is over. The line disbands. People stroll across the bridge toward the Conrad Hilton Hotel on Michigan Avenue.

Suddenly, without warning, the bridge is closed by the National Guard. With bayonets fixed, they order those who have not yet had time to cross "back into the park."

The soldiers are armed with rifles with fixed bayonets. The bayonets are now unsheathed. Others carry flame throwers filled with tear gas. Hundreds of other soldiers are deployed to seal off the spectators and the press from us and this is, for me, the most alarming maneuver of all. A group of soldiers have set up a B A R (Browning Automatic Rifle). It is loaded, and two extra boxes of ammunition are on hand. A young boy asks, "Do you plan to use that?" A soldier replies, "We will if we have to." The boy persists, "Why would you use it?" The soldier answers, "You people want to tear down all that they built," indicating the Chicago skyline behind him. I miss the youngster's answer as I walk north to the next

54

Suddenly, without warning, the bridge is closed by the National Guard.

A soldier responds with a blast of tear gas.

bridge. There a sun-tanned man in his early twenties is engaged in serious conversation with the soldiers. "I was in the Peace Corps in Columbia," he begins.

At the Balbo bridge a newsman displays his credentials but is turned back. "The Guardsman summoned a lieutenant. 'If I let anyone else across,' he said, 'I'm going to lose this bridge.' 'Lieutenant,' I said, 'I don't want your bridge. I just want to cross it.' He shrugged, muttered, 'Orders,' and walked away." The *National Observer.*

Communication with the soldiers has now almost ceased as they have put on their gas masks. I walk one block north in the hope of crossing the next bridge.

Just as I arrive, a young girl approaches a group of the soldiers. "It's going to be dark soon. We can't spend the night in the park. Why can't we go back into town?" A soldier responds with a blast of tear gas. "You pig," a man shouts at them. Another blast of gas.

The girl's face is burned by the gas. She chokes and cries, trying to catch her breath. She begins to vomit. I have not suffered a direct hit, but my eyes are affected. I am partially blinded and I have difficulty breathing.

A woman, not part of the demonstration, tries to drive her automobile across the bridge. A rifle with a fixed bayonet is pointed at her. She is incredulous. When the gas comes, she chokes and backs up her car.

"Just then, troops commanding the next bridge north sprayed its approach with tear gas, and I ran, choking, eyes and nose running, farther up the park. Halfway up there I hit another cloud of gas, much worse than the first." The *National Observer.*

We stand about in small and scattered groups, not

knowing where to go or what to do. There is no one even to surrender to. Any approach toward the bridge brings choking gas. Some of the youngsters are frustrated. Others confused. Some are almost angry. I am furious. I have seen enough this day.

I walk north another block, approach the soldiers with long and quick steps, flash a press pass from a Danish newspaper that I have written for and pass through the line. They don't question me, evidently thinking I know no English. I walk west to Michigan Avenue and then south toward the Hilton where I see thousands of demonstrators outraged at the police action. Some chant, "Sieg Heil, Sieg Heil," at the police and soldiers. Two hours before, I would have disapproved. Now, I do not. Thousands then shout, "Peace now. Peace now." I look about and study the faces that surround me. Many have swollen eyes and burned skin. Some have been clubbed, their shirts still wet with coagulating blood. One young man, dressed in army surplus O. D.'s, takes the microphone attached to a portable address system. He looks up at the towering hotels on Michigan Avenue that provide the western boundary for our battlefield. 'Do you see what has happened to us?" he shouts. "We came here to speak for peace. We want no trouble." A spectator standing at the base of a hotel shouts back, "Then why don't you go home?" The youth with the microphone appears unable to answer the question. Finally, the best he can do is to say, "We can't." I ponder the exchange as we walk south, now passing the Sheraton-Blackstone. Why do I not go home now? I turn to Carolyn Mugar, the photographer, and ask her if she wants to leave. "No," she answers. "Why?" I persist. "We can't," she answers as well.

## CHAPTER VI

# michigan avenue
# wednesday evening

The last time I was in Chicago it was in connection with the publication of a book I had written, and I stayed at the Hilton. How different Michigan Avenue looks from above. An eight lane, magnificent boulevard, running between the hotels on the west and the beautifully landscaped parks to the east, and beyond the parks, Lake Michigan. But now the police are brandishing clubs as we approach. The demonstrators begin to sing. We begin to sing. "Oh beautiful for spacious skies, for amber waves of grain . . ."

It is just before nightfall. Most of the demonstrators have found their way into Michigan Avenue directly in front of the Hilton. The more timid congregate in the parks, further from the police. Some have walked north and then south for miles to circumvent the National Guard on the bridges. Some, still suffering the effects of the gas, sit down in front of the Hilton.

Some, still suffering from the effect of the gas, sit down in front of the Hilton.

One young man carries a "Welcome to Chicago" sign upon which someone has superimposed a drawing of barbed wire.

It is 7:56, and without warning or apparent cause a mass of police charge into the demonstrators. I am in the front line and unable to understand what prompted the charge or even how the signal was given to the police.

61

It is 7:56 and without warning or apparent cause a mass of police charge into the demonstrators.

Some police swing the night sticks wildly, others hold both ends and push with it. An unmarked police car drives toward the seated demonstrators. I am just behind the car. An officer in front of me, and to my right, has just struck a woman with his club. Another, to my left, strikes a seated demonstrator over the head.

An officer in front of me and to my right has just struck a woman with his club. Another, to my left, strikes a seated demonstrator over the head.

Throughout the melee, Carolyn takes pictures. Two officers see her taking pictures and charge after her. She stands still, preparing her camera for another picture, as I grab her hand and try to drag her toward the park. "Get that camera," one cop yells. Another swings his club as Carolyn ducks. The club strikes a glancing blow to the

Another officer grabs for a camera but the owner moves
it away in time. The officer then grabs the camera equipment case.

camera. We run into the park with both officers in pursuit.
One shouts, "Halt." We run as fast as we can. Caroyln
was a high school field hockey star a few years ago and
I used to run in high school and play some basketball for
an Army team. Both officers are on the beefy side. A layer
of fat bulges over the belt of one. We escape. Carolyn
checks out the camera and it seems to be in good working
order.

To the police, the photographers are the enemy. Near

us another officer grabs for a camera but the owner moves it away in time. The officer then grabs the camera equipment case.

We stand on the edge of the park. All around us the police are chasing and beating the fleeing youngsters. Three cops charge toward us. We run deep into the park and escape again. The police charge up on the grass, chasing and clubbing those unable to run fast enough.

The police charge up on the grass, chasing and clubbing those unable to run fast enough.

One man has just been struck over the head and is being
hit again as he is driven to a waiting police van.

Once caught, the protestors are either beaten or arrested, often both. One man has just been struck over the head
and is being hit again as he is driven to a waiting police
van. We move in closer to take a picture. An officer raises
his club as he wheels toward us and we flee into the park
yet again.

## WEDNESDAY EVENING

A plainclothesman seizes a young man with one hand and strikes him over the head with a blackjack. I am standing ten feet away. The youngster crumples. The officer strikes him again over the head. The officer, blackjack still in his right hand, drags the man toward a police van. Carolyn takes a picture. An officer standing nearby sees her. The cop lunges at her and swings his club at the camera. He shouts, "Stop!" She snaps his pic-

A plainclothesman seizes a young man with one hand and strikes him over the head with a blackjack.

The cop lunges at her and swings his club at the camera.

ture and runs. He is too slow and heavy for genuine pursuit.

In a New York City office, George P. Hunt, managing editor of *Life* magazine, drafts a page-three Editors Note for the next issue. It is entitled, "A mystical fear of cameras." It is about Czechoslovakia.

We are deep in the park now, perhaps twenty-five yards from the police action. Several boys are bleeding profusely from head wounds. One girl writhes on her back and sobs. She is approximately seven months pregnant. An officer sprayed Chemical Mace into her face.

68

It is 7:57. The street is cleared . . . at least thirty-five having suffered serious head injuries in sixty seconds.

Her condition prevented her from running away fast enough. Her husband stands over her. He is almost berserk. "I'll kill them. If anything happens to our baby, I'll kill them," he shouts. An officer, standing near the curb looks up. A medical team arrives wearing white. The nurses are in long white coats with red cross armbands. The doctors and male medical students in white jackets and white trousers. They examine and treat the woman on the grass. Others move toward the boys who are bleeding. They begin to halt the flow of blood.

It is 7:57. The street is cleared. Just one minute has

passed since the police charge began. Many demonstrators have been injured, with at least thirty-five having suffered serious head injuries in sixty seconds.

The police have regrouped into ranks in front of the Hilton. Two medics carry the pregnant girl toward the police line and ask for permission to take her through, to a hospital. "Get back." an officer answers. "No one passes." A doctor replies intently, "Officer, she may be seriously injured and she is pregnant." The officer responds, "Get back, you." The doctor asked if an ambulance could be brought into the area to evacute the woman. The officer answers, "No. And get the fuck back. I'm not telling you again."

One medical student, dressed in white garb, walks south, toward the police lines, on the park side of the street. Two officers grab him, throw him down and begin to beat him.

The next day Hubert Humphrey condemned the demonstrators. "They came prepared," he said. "They came looking for trouble. They came with helmets. They even brought their own medical teams." Those wearing helmets were the police, the National Guard and news reporters and photographers with the networks and various newspapers. Perhaps less than two percent of the protestors wore helmets. In any event, a helmet is clearly a defensive, not an offensive device. Throughout the evening and for the next day, I wished that I too had come prepared with a helmet and sneakers.

The medical teams were not brought by the protesters although they too could hardly be classified as weapons of aggression. They organized themselves from the local medical schools in Chicago and from the Chicago Chapter of the Medical Committee for Human Rights. Long before the bloody week began the doctors and medical students met with the police and city officials to proclaim their neutrality and to explain their function—to provide aid to any one who may be injured, civilians or police officers. More than seventy-five percent of the medical personnel were from the Chicago area.

Dr. Thomas S. Harper wrote, in a letter published by the *New York Times,* "One medical student was set upon by several policemen, knocked to the ground and repeatedly struck with night sticks." He added, "The right of the ill and injured to prompt medical attention is recognized throughout the civilized world. The denial of this right by Mayor Daley and his police force constitutes a breach of human rights and a denial of the right of the medical profession to carry out its traditional functions." He said that "vehicles for evacuation of the wounded were denied access to the demonstration areas."

It is 7:58. The police march over the personal effects left behind by the fleeing demonstrators.

Shoes, sandals, a suitcase, sweaters, a McCarthy peace flower are left behind. Forming a back drop for the police advance, north on Michigan, is a sign of the Committee for Non-Violent Action from New England. It reads, "Make love, not war."

The police take up new positions in front of the Hilton. Within ten minutes the demonstrators are back.

The police march over the personal effects left behind by the fleeing demonstrators.

## WEDNESDAY EVENING

They chant:

"What do we want?"

"Peace."

"When do we want it?"

"Now."

Within ten minutes the demonstrators are back.

The police and the National Guard prepare for another charge.

Truck loads of National Guardsmen are brought into the street. The police and National Guard form lines. They prepare for another charge.

National Guard units stationed five minutes away at Wabash Avenue are called upon. They arrive with machine guns.

In the lull before the next charge, a police photographer takes pictures of those in the street and the park. Just after he takes my picture, Carolyn takes his.

National Guard units stationed five minutes away at Wabash Avenue are called upon. They arrive with machine guns. A police photographer takes pictures of those in the street and the park.

A mule wagon from the deep south drives onto Michigan Avenue. It is part of Rev. Ralph Abernathy's Poor Peoples march. One senior officer waves the wagon onward. In a moment, another officer fires tear gas at the wagon. The mules almost panic. The elderly driver, partially blinded by the gas, has trouble controlling them. His younger companions, their faces set in sorrow and disbelief, try to assist him. In the background, a sign reads, "Welcome to Chicago." At the Democratic convention, five miles away, the band strikes up—"Happy Days Are Here Again."

Television reporters move toward the wagon. One girl says, "We had less trouble in Mississippi." An officer explains, "We were trying to help. We just wanted to separate you from this crowd." A man on the wagon looks up and answers, "We are all black."

Suddenly, another police charge. They come from the south, swinging clubs. They pursue those least able to escape. A crippled man with a cane is knocked down and clubbed. I run, this time, toward the hotel side of the street, to the safety of the spectators. But there is no safety there. The police are beating spectators as well. The police drive a number of spectators toward a large glass window. A club strikes me in the right kidney. Men and women flee in panic, pressing up against a restaurant window. The glass breaks. A woman falls through the broken window onto the glass. The police continue to

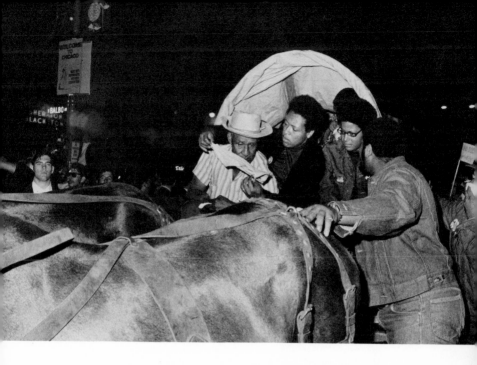

A mule train from the deep south drives onto Michigan Avenue . . . an officer fires tear gas at the wagon.

charge, clubs flailing. They run through the broken window and beat the woman on the floor and the others who have run there to seek shelter.

"Suddenly, for no reason that I could discern, a wedge of police lunged toward a crowd of bystanders who had been watching the melee from behind a police barricade. Clubs flying, the police plunged into the crowd,

An officer, under the careful scrutiny of his superior officer, picks up a wooden horse and hurls it into the crowd.

which recoiled toward the hotel's facade. The pressure of dozens of bodies against the glass shattered two windows and a door of the Haymarket Inn, a hotel bistro on the Conrad Hilton's northeast corner. Several people, women included, fell through the glass onto the fragments inside. Police followed them in, clubs flailing." The *National Observer*.

I run further north, still keeping to the hotel side of Michigan. But the police were there, two blocks from the Hilton, clubbing citizens who had just gone out for a walk.

"As the battle raged on Michigan Avenue, policemen appeared to be belting everyone in sight. Several well-dressed women were crying hysterically." The *Chicago Daily News*.

I cross over toward the park. A plainclothes officer tears down a McCarthy sign. Several at the edge of the crowd, standing on the sidewalk respond, "Oink, oink." The officer, under the careful watch of his superior officer, picks up a wooden horse and hurls it into the crowd.

The officer charges onto the sidewalk, and assisted by his superior, drags a man toward a police van. The

The officer charges onto the sidewalk and assisted by his superior drags a man toward a police van.

formal charge could only be, "Oinking at a police officer in the performance of his duty." Other officers charge into the crowd, evidently after one man in particular. They catch him. They beat him repeatedly with clubs about the head and body. His eyeglasses are smashed.

"Prof. Sidney M. Peck was downed by other policemen a hundred feet away. He was taken to the Bridewell Hospital, where he was found to be suffering from a possible skull fracture, possible fractured finger and possible dislocated shoulder." The *Chicago Daily News.*

In the editorial offices of the *New York Daily News* on 42nd Street, a rather detached and simplistic view of the events was taken. "In this instance, police could choose between keeping order as best they might and letting the mob run wild. They chose the former. Only a commy or a complete kook, we believe, would say they chose wrongly." Yet in the same newspaper, on the same day that this editorial which questioned the loyalty or sanity of those critical of the police performance, veteran *Daily News* reporter William Federici wrote, "Chicago cops use the doctrine of pursuit of people, clubbing them all the way, maybe for blocks." Another *Daily News* reporter wrote from Chicago, "It was in fact a police riot."

Suddenly, without discernable reason or warning, just as it began, the police riot ended. We moved cautiously back toward the Hilton. One block north of the Hilton became liberated territory. We moved into the streets. The police and the Guard withdrew to the west side of Michigan Avenue. Then they advanced to the east, across the street, leaving the park and the east sidewalk accessible to the demonstrators. We moved into the park and onto the sidewalk directly across from the hotel. The medics were busy. Scores were bleeding or unable to walk. No all-inclusive total of those injured can be known. For example, no record was made of my injury, which continued to cause considerable pain. Broken bones and serious head wounds were treated. Other less serious, and more numerous, injuries were ignored. Men and women had watched the police charges from the windows of the Hilton, which, being the largest hotel in the world, accommodates many windows. Many people still looked out onto the street from that hotel and from the Sheraton-Blackstone one block north.

What do they think up there, we wondered? Can they see that we have committed no crimes? Can they see what the police have done? Then a chant begins from the crowd, directed to the hotel windows. "Blink your lights. Blink your lights. If you support us, blink your lights." In a moment, scores of lights in the Hilton and the Blackstone began blinking. The demonstrators burst into a spontaneous roar of approval. Kids with blood splattered shirts, girls with burned faces, stand in the park and on the sidewalk, just feet away from ranks of cops brandishing their clubs, and applaud, with their faces raised in gratitude and hope. They had not come to destroy. They had come to find something positive to hold on to. They had come to find the best of America, not even knowing that they, themselves, were the best we have produced.

They had discovered the worst as well, as we were reminded again and again. Someone from the back of the crowd, from the safety of the darkness in the park, hurled an empty plastic container into the street, then another. They had evidently been used by the medics to carry water in for treatment of tear gas burns. From the demonstrators came the cry, "No. No. No." But it was too late. Another police charge began. This one, perhaps because it was a reaction to a form of provocation, was the most savage yet. I was in the front line when the charge broke. An officer swung his stick at me in a murderous blow. I ducked and it missed. It was so close that it brushed past my hair. I felt at the time that if it had hit me it might have been a serious or even fatal blow. He abandoned me as I ran north again. I looked back to see him smash a man in the leg and a woman in the kidney area. He saw me and I ran again.

"I had just run to another *National Observer* reporter's corner room, which commanded a panoramic view of the scene below, when all hell broke loose in the street. Police charged in groups into the protesters, who surged in waves in all directions, trying to escape. No one was immune; women, bystanders, several ministers, even one crippled man who could not hobble fast enough with his cane, all were clubbed and kicked, some more than once, by the police." The *National Observer*.

We are driven north two blocks by the officers. Now the crowd, primarily to the north of us, begins to run south toward us. The National Guard has flanked the demonstrators and spectators and is driving them back toward the officers' flailing clubs. Many in the crowd panic. They don't know which way to run. Only one portable bull horn is left. The police have stolen the others. A leader holds it and says, "Please, be calm. It is our desire to disperse if they will let us." Someone shouts, "Yeah, let's be calm. And let's have a pray-in for the cops, too." From the bull horn, "Please, stay calm. We are trying to find out what they want." Voice from the crowd: "We know what they want. They want to kill us."

The Guard stops advancing. The police begin to fall back and to regroup. We stand in the street, near the parkside curb, and very close to a concrete divider wall built as part of a ramp for underground parking. A police officer in a three-wheel motorcycle drives at a reckless speed off the bridge, makes a sharp right turn and appears to be aiming for us. I leap onto the curb and lean against the concrete wall. Carolyn is to my right and on the curb as well. A frail blonde girl to my left climbs onto the curb but falls off as the motorcycle reaches her. She screams and I reach for her. She grabs onto me and almost makes it. The motorcycle has struck her leg a glancing blow. Another cycle follows. All three of us press against the wall.

The girl is in pain. She half stumbles, half falls off the curb, but now officers are clearing the street with swinging clubs. One swings at her. I pull her toward me and the club strikes my back, directly on my spine, just above my belt. I hear the club strike Carolyn next. I cannot restrain myself. I face him and shout, "You son-of-a-bitch. This girl's hurt." He raises his club, says, "Fuck you," and turns without striking another blow. A doctor picks up the girl and carries her toward a park bench. We are now being chased from the north and from the south. We flee to a bridge to escape toward the lake, but the Guard is waiting there with gas masks and gas guns. They fire at us. My eyes tear and I begin to choke again. A doctor hurries over and shouts, "Take short breaths. Just take short breaths. Do not rub your eyes. You can cause permanent damage if you do." As we try to escape from the tear gas, police officers begin the chase again.

Now police arrive from the west carrying shotguns. Others run in front of them swinging clubs. A man struck

As we try to escape from the tear gas, police officers begin the chase again.

over the shoulder and he falls. Two cops, one Negro, one white, begin to beat him. Standing very near me, a long-haired boy shouts at the cops, "You mother-fucking Judas." The two officers leave the now unconscious demonstrator in the street and joined by another Negro cop, they chase the long-haired youth. One officer shouts, "I'll kill you." Another screams, "Get him, kill him." I am terrified that the lad will be caught. The three officers

They fill the street again and walk back to the hotel singing America the Beautiful.

appear to be insane at this moment. I want to help but I am frustrated by the fear that I can do nothing. The young man runs onto the bridge. The Guard is at the other end. One Negro cop reaches the steps of the bridge first. He is running too fast to negotiate the steps. He falls and smashes his face into the concrete. The other cops stop and pick him up. They help him back toward the police concentration. He looks like a football hero being carried back to his bench. I follow at a discreet distance. A reporter asks, "What happened?" The white officer answers, "One of those bastards threw a rock at him."

For ten years I have been a follower of Gandhi. I forget that now. I am consumed with hatred for the police, for their use of naked force against the defenseless, against women and cripples. I think of how I might retaliate.

But now the attacks have subsided again. The kids, driven more than two blocks north of the Hilton by the gas and the clubs, fill the street again and walk back to the hotel. They sing *America the Beautiful* as they walk.

We are back again.

We fill the park across from the Hilton. We sing and we chant. We know that we may be clubbed again and gassed again. But we know as well that we will be back again. The chant begins, "The streets belong to the people." And then, "Peace now. Peace now."

Five miles away, the balloting starts. Portable radios carry the news into the park. One lad with long hair holds an American flag aloft. Whenever a state casts a sizeable vote for McCarthy, he waves the flag back and forth enthusiastically. When Humphrey receives the required number of votes, the youngster lowers the flag and then flies it upside down. *Chicago's American* published a picture of the flag as proof that the demonstrators were disloyal and were expressing "disdain for their country." The *National Observer* commented, "For ships at sea, a nation's flag flown upside down is the international signal of distress."

Volunteers for Sen. McCarthy set up a first aid station in the 15th floor suite of the senator's headquarters in the Hilton. The volunteers gave up their own passes to enable injured persons to pass through the cordon around the hotel. McCarthy visited the injured to speak with those suffering from bleeding wounds on the head, broken bones and serious bruises. One girl sobbed almost hysterically. The senator was shaken, his face gray and his jaw set. He congratulated his staff, praised them for establishing the impromptu clinic and said, "This is the way we will go on from here."

Ten floors above the clinic, Hubert Humphery entered his suite. When an aide opened a window, he complained of the smell of tear gas.

The delegates begin to return to the Hilton in buses. Some buses carry McCarthy posters. The demonstrators cheer them. After the delegates had time to return to their rooms, the chant begins in the park again. "Blink your lights. Blink your lights. If you support us, blink your lights." Many windows flash the sign of support to the

We signaled peace and cheered the delegates.

demonstrators in the park. We signal peace and cheer
the delegates. A middle-aged man wearing *Associated
Press* credentials, standing but a few feet from me, begins
to cry.

# CHAPTER VII

# the mccarthy delegates march thursday afternoon

Thursday morning Donald Peterson, the Chairman of the Wisconsin delegation to the convention, announced that he was going to walk to the Amphitheatre. He invited delegates and others to join him. He said that the walk was in protest against the brutality evidenced by the police and National Guard units the night before which had prevented demonstrators from marching to the convention hall. The walk is set for four that afternoon.

At exactly four, Peterson began his walk. Several hundred who supported McCarthy—delegates, clergymen, nuns and honored guests and their wives and others—are present. They began at the Bismarck Hotel in the downtown section of the city. Only two police officers are visible. The marchers wear ties and short hair.

As we proceed east on Randolph Street, two demonstrators from yesterday's march join the walk. They are long-haired; one carries a sleeping roll.

At 4 p.m. the delegates and friends begin their walk.

There is no police effort to interfere with the walk. Two well-dressed men stand with two police officers at the corner of Randolph and Clark. One of the men shouts, "You are a bunch of mother-fuckers." Three nuns walking together turn away. One delegate looks back in disbelief at the men. The two officers are smiling as the man shouts, "You heard me, Jew." A friendly ob-

Two demonstrators from yesterday join the walk.

server, walking along, remarks that "this sure is an easy march." A member of the clergy answers severely, "A walk. This is not a march. It is a walk." The observer replies, "Father, semantics won't save you from the Chicago cops."

At East Monroe and Michigan we pass hundreds of the wounded and other veterans of yesterday's assaults. They stand and applaud. They begin the chant, "The streets belong to the people." Someone in the line answers, "Join us," and as they do, the line increases in size and becomes more diversified in terms of dress. Soon the march stretches over many blocks.

Soon the march stretches over many blocks.

It is a bright sunny day. The young people have found what they came to Chicago seeking. Some establishment middle-aged delegates are with them. The walk leadership frowns upon chanting or singing so the youngsters hum the *Star Spangled Banner*. It is 4:20 and we turn east off Michigan onto Adams. At the corner we meet hundreds of cheering young people. Many carry sleeping bags or blankets. Many wear bandages. They cheer the delegates at the head of the line and then join in at the end. We walk past a barber shop. Inside, a customer in his early fifties is having his hair cut. A boy shouts out to him, "Join us." He smiles at the youngster and his hand comes out from under the barber's cloth draped from around his neck. He holds up two fingers in a "V."

It is 4:30 and we pass State and Congress where two officers are directing traffic. Good naturedly, a girl says to them, "Why I hardly recognize you without your gas mask." Two young men have a different greeting for the police officers: "Oink." A bus driving north passes us as we walk south on State. The youngsters shout, "Scab," at the bus driver. An unauthorized bus strike led by the black members of the union is taking place. The delegates are unaware of the strike and when told what the young people are shouting about, one says, betraying some exasperation, "Can't they just worry about one thing at a time? We are not here for that." But to the demonstrators, all of the issues are relevant. They want to end the war in Viet Nam, construct a representative Democratic Party, work for justice for the blacks and a decent living for all workers. To them these goals are inseparable. There is but one issue—everything. The bus stop to let off some passengers, and the demonstrators call to riders, "Don't ride the bus. Walk with us."

It is 4:33 as we pass the headquarters of the Chicago Police Department on State Street. The McCarthy delegates at the head of the line either ignore it or fail to notice it. The young people cheer as they pass. The police guarding the building appear stunned. Some in the walk call out to them, "Join us."

At 4:50 as we near 14th Street, a Negro wearing an undershirt and driving a huge red truck looks up, takes one hand off the wheel and flashes a peace sign. The kids cheer.

Moments later, workers lean out of the Department of Public Aid building and applaud the marchers.

The mood could not be happier. A young man with a bandaged head turns to a girl and says, "It was all worth it."

But as we pass 15th Street, we see a row of police officers blocking the sidewalk, clubs in their hands.

Within moments hundreds of additional police arrive

95

A row of police officers blocking the sidewalk, clubs in their hands.

on the scene. Peterson walks up to the police, who prevent the walk from continuing. He asks, "Is there anything wrong with walking on the sidewalks of Chicago? Is it some kind of a crime? If not, we'd like to pass now."

"You can't go on," a patrolman replies. "Why not?" Peterson asks. "Those are orders," is the reply.

While Peterson is awaiting the arrival of someone with whom he can have an exchange, the National Guard arrives.

Peterson walks up to the police.
The National Guard arrives.

In a sense I was a war correspondent.

Two Deputy Police Chiefs also arrive. Chief Nygren tells Peterson, "This march constitutes a threat to the security of the city." When Peterson inquires how that can be so, the Chief answers, "I'm running the police force." The delegates plead with the officers under a hot sun.

Before long some of the delegates remove their jackets. A police officer insists that he is just following orders.

A lawyer reminds him that Eichmann used a similar defense. The lawyer for the delegation speaks of the Constitution and of the rights of American citizens.

The delegates plead with the officers under a hot sun.

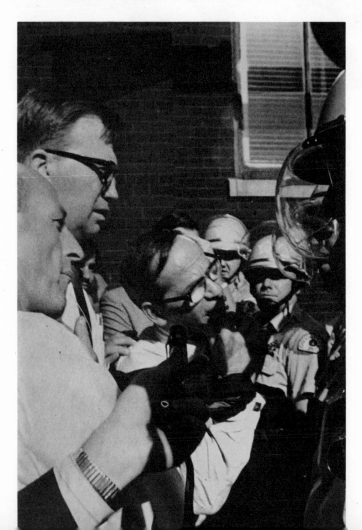

We are discontinuing the walk in the interest of avoiding further injuries.

A *UPI* reporter and a radio correspondent listen. Suddenly Lt. Mahoney pushes them back violently. The *UPI* man stands his ground and asks, "Who are you going to try to hurt now?"

The attorney for the delegation advises Peterson that "this constitutes the rawest denial of due process that I have ever seen. It is outrageous. It is un-American. But in the interest of peace and in order to avoid having anyone hurt, I think that we should turn back." Peterson reluctantly agrees that there is nothing else that can be done. Peterson, holding a bull horn, stands up on the base of a stanchion and announces that "we are discontinuing the walk in the interest of avoiding further injuries."

By now the line of marchers extends many hundreds of yards. Only those toward the front can hear Peterson's words. They greet them with, "No. We are not turning around." A dozen dramas are acted out simultaneously. Some of the youngsters want to communicate the decision to those further back in the line. They set out to pass the word. One bearded, well-dressed youth walks disgustedly away, turns his head toward the delegates and says, "You liberals can always be counted on—to cop out. But when will *we* ever learn that."

A chubby girl on the verge of tears reaches out to grab his arm and says, "That's not fair. They didn't have to come out on the street with us. You should praise them, not attack them." A half dozen other youths nod in agreement, while most stand in puzzlement.

A few reporters and some of the youngsters crowd into the street, just off the curb, to hear the discussion that takes place at the head of the line. One boy of about sixteen begins to cry as he talks to a delegate's wife. "We can't leave. Don't you see that?" he says.

"I know, I know," she answers.

Now the tears are streaming down his face. "Don't you know me?" he asks. "I worked for you, for McCarthy, in Wisconsin. If you leave us here alone with the cops we'll be beaten again."

She begins to cry. She turns to her husband, "We brought them here. We can't leave them here."

The man is clearly worried, his face lined with conflict. With him are his two small children. He begins to walk toward the back of the line with his wife. A few, including a wounded veteran of yesterday's war, (or was it the day before?) begin to chant, "Liberals go home."

An elderly man walks up to the delegate and his wife. "If you leave these kids alone with the police, you take the responsibility for what happens."

The delegate answers, "Look, I'm no leader. Why does everyone talk to me?" But he knows that he has not answered the question to his own satisfaction.

Deputy Police Chief Riordan sees some of us standing just off the curb. He screams, "Get up on the sidewalk," and as he does, police officer Salvato roughly pushes me and others with his club. A reporter is prodded by another officer, and he writes down the officer's name. I think back to point three of the agreement with the media executives. "Officers of at least lieutenant rank" will be assigned to "assure protection of the rights of the press and of bystanders." I question our capacity to rely upon Riordan if the clubs begin to swing this sunny afternoon at 16th and State. The word has now reached further into the line. The derisive "Liberals go home" is replaced with an almost pleading "Don't leave us. Don't leave us."

The delegate returns to the head of the line with his wife. He has deposited the two children somewhere. A young boy says, "Thank you for coming back." He answers, "We never left."

My notebook reveals a score of different conversations as ministers, delegates, the convention's honored guests, wrestle with their own consciences and explain what must be done to their bedraggled army of volunteers. A young man walks up to a delegate. "Sir, may I talk with you for a moment?" A wife to a delegate: "We are not leaving. I don't care what happens; we can't leave if they stay here." The response: "Oh, are the kids deciding for us now?" Answer: "Yes."

A boy to a cop: "What do you mean you're 'gung-ho'? Do you mean you like to hit people?" The cop to the boy: "Maybe."

A delegate to a girl: "You know I never contracted to lead this march. I don't know if I'm contributing anything by staying here."

Another delegate to another girl: "I don't want anyone hurt because of my decision."

A minister to a group of young men and women: "We have made our demonstration. Now we can leave. We have won."

Voices: "How, by turning back?"

"I won't turn back."

"Where is Martin Luther King? He would not have left us."

"We don't want anyone injured. We feel responsible."

"We have been injured."

"Injured? We're willing to die. This is for our country."

"Were you there last night?"

"No. I was at the convention hall voting for McCarthy."

"What would you tell the Czech people? We love our country too, and we're not turning it over to the pigs."

"Sellouts."

"The delegates did not sell us out. It took courage for them to come on this march."

"Where are they going now that the pigs are here?"

104

"The police have agreed to let us walk closer to the Amphitheatre. But the delegates will feel morally free to pass through the police lines. Do you agree?"

"The delegates can do whatever they want. This is our country and we're not turning back."

It is 5:50 and reinforcements from the National Guard arrive in a dozen trucks. A full colonel leads them. One Guardsman looks about quickly, then flashes the familiar "V" for peace sign from behind his M-1. A hundred demonstrators return it.

The exchange continues at the front of the line, but suddenly it has become academic. The demonstration is over. Those toward the rear of the line have turned around and are walking east, toward the Hilton. Word has reached them that McCarthy and Gregory are speaking in the street there.

# CHAPTER VIII

# thursday evening

It is not yet dark and I decide to wander around deep behind the police lines before returning to the Hilton area. Using my Danish press pass, I become a reporter again, and continue on to 16th Street, where I walk east, toward Michigan Avenue. There I see, for the first time, a tank-like armored vehicle with a thirty calibre machine gun mounted atop it. It's surrounded by soldiers, some carrying automatic weapons. It lumbers slowly behind police lines, but toward the demonstrators. Its giant treads chew up the Chicago streets.

I walk north toward the hotel and note that traffic is tied up for blocks due to the presence of the tank. Literally hundreds of motorists honk their horns. Finally the city, or at least one portion of it, is entirely tied up; but the demonstrators are too far away to take solace from the scene.

I arrive at the park across from the Hilton, and McCarthy has just finished speaking. Wiping a tear from his eye, he has promised never to compromise with what he has seen in Chicago. He is given a huge ovation by the demonstrators. It is clear that he is their hero.

Pierre Salinger wants to speak. Some remember his support of Lyndon Johnson and his complete commitment

It lumbers slowly behind police lines, but toward the demonstrators.

to the war in Viet Nam, and suggest that he take his cigar and leave. Before doing so, however, he invites them to join the Democratic Party, which has been so useful to him. There is little response, a few boos, but most feel him to be too irrelevant to bother with. A doctor wearing medical whites speaks next. He explains that he does not support the demonstrators; that he and the other members of the medical teams are neutral and that they have been

I would like to invite you to my house this evening.

willing to treat both sides. A few chuckle, knowing that few officers have sustained injuries and that they were immediately and well cared for by the city's regular emergency facilities. The audience listens with little interest in the speaker but with respect for what he and his colleagues have tried to do on the Chicago battlefield. Some applaud when he is through.

Gregory, who had introduced McCarthy and who had spoken earlier, has a short message to deliver. For days the police authorities had made it clear that any attempt to march toward the Amphitheatre, due south, would be repulsed with force. Greg speaks: "You young people are all my friends, and so I would like to invite you to my house this evening. It's south of here. The address is 1451 East 55th Street and it's apartment 1030. I'm going to start walking there in just a few minutes and I'd be pleased if you would like to walk along with me. Now the fuzz has been acting a little strange lately, so they might try to interfere. You just tell them that you're going to visit me. They might arrest you. I don't care if they want to arrest me for walking home. No one, no one, is gonna turn me 'round. Oh, one second, there's someone here from the Justice Department who says that a couple of generals want to talk with me. Why don't you all wait here for a few minutes while I talk with them? No need to worry though, I'll be walking with you in a few minutes."

The more than three thousand young people, with just a scattering of blacks, listen intently as they are advised that they may be arrested. As if to underscore that danger, National Guard units and Chicago police reinforcements arrive. Without apparent exception, the demonstrators agree to walk with Gregory.

Greg's conference with the generals lasts more than a few minutes. They ask him to reconsider. "Reconsider what," he asks? "Walking home in my own town? What's happening to this country?" But he knows the answer to his question. "Look, I want no violence."

An officer responds, indicating the crowd, "Tell that to them."

Gregory answers, "Look here, you know that they're not the cause of any violence. Anyway, you push people too far and you are going to see some violence for the first time from them. I am non-violent. I am also a vegetarian. But I don't tell other people how to act. I wouldn't knock a forkful of steak out of your mouth just because it's against my principles to eat meat. And I don't tell Stokley and Rap Brown how to act neither. You just let us go for a walk and there will be peace. Or arrest us and there still will be peace. But if you attack, why that's violence."

Unable to persuade him to abandon the walk, the generals agree that the demonstrators will be allowed to

110

They listen intently.

proceed for awhile. If the time comes that the officials decide that the marchers are too close to the convention, the Guard will halt the march. But there will be no gas and no violence. Those who wish to proceed will be arrested as the Guard will let them through, to walk into waiting police vans.

Gregory and I walk together, south on Michigan, as three
thousand follow.

Gregory reports back to the more than three thousand waiting in the park. He warns them that they may
be arrested. Greg and I walked south on Michigan together, as three thousand follow.

Blocks away, the National Guard calls for reinforcements. Army two-and-one-half ton trucks, filled with armed
troops, converge on 18th and Michigan.

# THURSDAY EVENING

A tank-like armored vehicle moves into position at the intersection.

The police have been called in off the street. Very few can be seen as the units of the Guard have taken over supervision of this march. Some of the younger veterans view this as a hopeful sign. I am less sanguine about the change and begin to consider the relative merits of each group of assailants.

Armed troops converge on 18th and Michigan Avenue.

In the first place, they are armed differently. The Guardsmen carry rifles, some have automatic weapons and sidearms. All have gas masks, some have gas guns, others have launchers for firing tear gas cannisters. I presume, I certainly hope, that the rifles are unloaded.

The police wear loaded pistols, some carry shotguns. All of them brandish sticks or clubs, and some carry Mace cans.

The police are better trained. Therefore, when they decide to club children, for example, they are more efficient at it. This is not said to slight the Guardsmen, but a club that can be swung with one hand is far easier to wield than a rifle, which requires both hands.

The rifle butt can be a deadly weapon, as I recall from my days of basic training in the Army, my memory refreshed by the events of the last two days. But it has a much shorter range than a night stick. With a fixed bayonet, however, its range and effectiveness are greatly enhanced.

If you are curious to know the name of the gentleman who is about to beat you or gas you, you might lean toward the police. If they have forgotten to violate their own regulations, they will be wearing a name plate and a badge number. The National Guard does not provide such easy identification for its enforcers.

Many of the Guardsmen have no stomach for the

fight; unlike the cops, they did not enlist to charge into their fellow Americans, and therefore, they appear to prefer the less personal weapon of gas to hand to hand combat. They are nervous, however, and more prone to start a riot without having had that intention. The police are much more enthusiastic about their work. They seem reluctant to utilize gas too early in the fray; it makes clubbing more difficult, as many of the officers do not wear masks. Also, it may annoy the tourists and interfere with the ordinary operations of commerce—the storekeepers who pay them each week. Of course, the spraying of Mace directly into the face is not against the rules.

My advice to you then, is largely dependent upon your own peculiarities. If you suffer from emphysimia, asthma or some other serious respiratory ill, tear gas could prove permanently harmful, or even fatal. Your best bet might be to hang around the police and risk a cracked skull, which, while painful, is rarely fatal. On the other hand, if you are in reasonably good health and in some profession where facial scars might render you less valuable, an area policed by the National Guard is for you. If you are fast, equipped with sneakers, and possess rather good peripheral vision, a street not too far from a police concentration might be a good choice. Do you recall ever having seen a thin Chicago cop?

If you are a bit older and slower and not an almost perfect specimen, better stay home and let your children

115

cope with today's realities. Should you be overcome by a desire to express yourself in the open air, you might consider a trip to Scandinavia, England, or for some, but not total relief, Spain.

The mood is not jubilant as we walk along, but neither is it oppressive. We expect no violence on this trip. Those who wish to carry their protest through to its conclusion will be arrested. Those who wish to turn back when the moment arrives may do so. I think as I walk along that very likely no one in our line of march is motivated to initiate violence; that in all probability, there need have been no confrontation at all if Mayor Daley had just relaxed the park curfew on Sunday instead of waiting to do it on Tuesday, and if we had been permitted an orderly march to within sight of the convention hall.

We pass 17th Street, still walking south on Michigan, and see the Army ahead. Eighteenth Street is barricaded. Thousands of soldiers are there. They are supported by armor, rifles with bayonets and automatic weapons. In front of them, jeeps strung across with barbed wire confront us.

By now some twenty-five delegates to the convention have joined us. Their badges provide immunity from arrest—for them. At 18th Street we are forced to halt. A general wants to talk to Greg again. As in days of old, the sea—this time comprised of helmeted, armed soldiers—opens up; Greg passes through and he disappears as it unites again.

He is taken to the waiting car with a waiting general. He is gone so long this time, some speculate that he may have been kidnapped. One delegate reports, "We can walk through to the convention without being arrested.

Jeeps strung across with barbed wire confront us.

The officer has said that all we have to do is show our convention badge. Let's go." Another suggests that they all just leave, and he starts to act out his own suggestion. Rev. Richard Neuhaus, a delegate from Brooklyn, speaks: "Our intention is to walk to the Amphitheatre. The police and the guard agree that we have the right to do that, but they do not agree that Dick Gregory has a right to invite guests to his house. I do not believe that this is equal treatment under the law. So I suggest we stay here with our friends." The move to abandon the marchers is halted.

Greg returns at 9:00 p.m. to announce that we can go no farther without being arrested. He adds, "They say that if I go through the line again, they will arrest me. I'm going now. See you later." He walks forward, the sea parts once more and once more closes in behind him. The police, waiting in the intersection with two patrol vans, arrest him.

A delegate suggests that the point has been made by Gregory's arrest and that "we may as well head home now." Murray Kempton, a journalist and a delegate from New York, who has been standing patiently at the very front of the line, turns toward the delegates and says, "Hell, I'm taking off my badge and going to dinner with Mr. Gregory."

He places his badge in his pocket, steps forward and

118

Murray Kempton says, "Hell, I'm taking off my badge and going to dinner with Mr. Gregory."

is arrested. Almost every delegate removes his badge and states that he is willing to be arrested. The police make the arrest very slowly. Rev. Neuhaus is arrested. So is Rev. James Meyer, a Catholic priest from Pontiac, Michigan. Now the police take Harris Woffard into custody. He is president of the State University of New York and a former White House aide.

119

A paraplegic veteran of World War II, in a wheel chair,
asked to be placed at the front of the line.

It is now 9:20 and only a handful have been placed
in the vans. Thomas Frazer, a paraplegic World War
II veteran in a wheel chair, has asked to be placed at
the front of the line. He is a delegate from Oklahoma.
He explains that he hopes his presence will discourage
any physical attack upon the young people. He removes
his badge, attempts to wheel himself across the street,
and is arrested. Rumor has it that he is an independ-

The crowd chants "We'll walk to jail."

ently wealthy man. In court that evening, the judge, ill-impressed by the fact that the defendant wears no tie, asks what bail he can post. He replies, "Why you just make it easy on yourself, judge." The judge is incredulous and annoyed and suggests a rather high bail. The defendant smiles and replies, "Are you sure that's enough?" as he takes out a roll of bills to offer cash bail.

An hour has passed and very few have been arrested.

A National Guard officer takes a bull horn to announce that if "anyone else steps forward he will be arrested." Everyone steps forward. The crowd chants, "Arrest us all. Arrest us all." For the first time the authorities realize that all three thousand are ready to go to jail. They are confused. They have brought but two vans. The crowd begins to shout, "We'll walk to jail. We'll walk to jail."

Now the atmosphere is charged. The tension mounts once it becomes clear that the authorities will not arrest those present and will not permit them to move ahead.

Carolyn and I stood at the very front of the line at this point. We saw the cause of the riot that ensued. The pictures that accompany this sequence are, to my knowledge, unique. They show the anatomy of a riot. One member of the Guard appeared to go berserk.

I was standing but a few feet from him.

He begins to mumble something, and then screams. Then he begins to charge toward the crowd.

Even his fellow soldiers seemed concerned by his unprovoked attack upon a demonstrator.

Just as it appears that a serious disturbance is likely to take place, a lieutenant steps forward from the rear ranks, orders the soldier back into formation and prevents a physical confrontation.

Moments later the soldier breaks ranks again, menaces

One member of the guard (far right) appeared to go berserk. He began to charge toward the crowd.

His fellow soldiers seemed concerned by his unprovoked attack upon a demonstrator.

a young couple with his rifle, turns toward me, wheels back toward the couple and strikes one of them with the rifle. The young man with the girl pushes back and another guardsman moves in, swinging his rifle.

Suddenly the command "Gas" is given. The soldiers retreat a few steps and put on gas masks while we stand

A lieutenant stepped forward from the rear ranks and ordered the soldier back into formation. Moments later the soldier broke ranks again, menaced young couple and then struck one of them with his rifle.

Suddenly the command "Gas" was given.

there facing the soldiers, not quite believing that it will end this way—not after all the assurance. Later, the general was to say that he did not give the order for gas. But it was gas, nevertheless.

At this point in the narrative, unlike the previous portions, in which I have relied heavily upon copiously written contemporaneous notes filling four notebooks, I rely entirely upon my memory. My recollection is sufficiently vivid, however.

## THURSDAY EVENING

The gas exploded on me. This is my first experience with a direct hit. My lungs immediately feel as if they are frozen, as if I tried to breathe in sub-zero weather. Within a second, I am gasping for breath. I remember the warning, "Take short breaths." But there is no air, just gas. I feel that I will suffocate if I don't breathe deeply. I am blinded. I am totally blind for the first time in my life. My eyes burn and I feel that tears are running down my face. My nose burns and also runs. I can not catch

We stand there facing the soldiers.

my breath. I can hardly speak. I try to say, "Are you all right, Carolyn?" and hear her say that she is blinded.

"Don't touch your eyes," I say, as I grab her hand and we run in what we hope is a northerly direction. I stumble as my feet strike someone stretched out in the street. Then we hear the Guard move up toward us. I can not see them, but I hear them coming closer. I hear a rifle butt strike flesh and bone very near to me.

"Are you all right?" I ask again. "Yes, are you?" she answers.

We hear screaming ahead of us along with the explosion of more tear gas cannisters. We are all running from the area as quickly as we can. The firing of tear gas into those in front of us is purely punitive and hardly designed to hasten our departure. Within a moment, we are forced to run through additional concentrations of the gas in order to escape being bludgeoned by the rifle-swinging guardsmen.

We run, blindly and crying, from the advancing soldiers. The exertion caused by running forces us to breathe more deeply, but our lungs burn intolerably and feel as if they will burst. We run on, hoping for some fresh air. I crash into a post of some kind in what was total darkness for me. At 16th Street we pause.

A voice commands, "Open your eyes." I try to as a stream of fluid washes over my face. Yet even at this I

128

Medics pour water into the eyes of those gassed.

was evidently unsuccessful for the voice repeats, with some annoyance, "Damn it, open your eyes. We don't have any water to spare." I open them. Within seconds I can see again, although my vision remains blurred for some time.

I lead Carolyn to the medic and her eyes are also washed of the toxic substance. As soon as her eyes clear, she takes a picture of the medics pouring water in the next patient's eyes.

Three medics kneel over a girl stretched out in the street. They had carried her from 17th Street. She had stopped breathing, in what appeared to be a traumatic

Two medics help a young man, bleeding from the head and mouth.

response to the gas. They begin artificial respiration. One doctor shouts at her, "Breathe, damn it, breathe." She starts to gasp and the doctor sighs with relief. Now she is breathing regularly. But another tear gas cannister explodes thirty feet from us. The medics help her up and help carry her, trying to escape the spreading gas.

A network television crew, wearing gas masks and helmets, is on the scene to question a demonstrator.

Two medics help a young man bleeding from the head and mouth to get away from the gas.

Another man, bleeding from the scalp, is aided by a medic. Water washes the gas from his eyes. A network television crew, wearing gas masks and helmets, is on the scene to interview him.

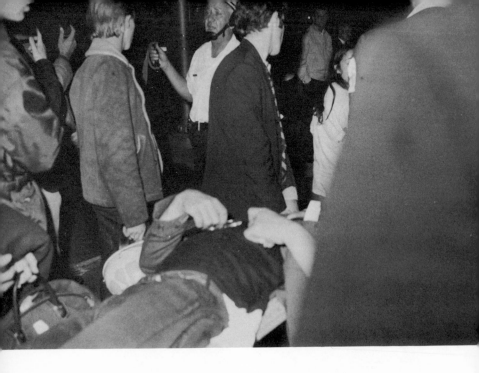

Another, beaten unconscious, is carried off on a stretcher, while a police officer, club raised, watches.

Another, beaten unconscious, is carried off on a stretcher while a police officer, club raised, watches.

We are tired now, near exhaustion. Many are vomiting in the street. The gas has not affected me that way yet. Several people come from an alley into which they ran to escape the fumes. A girl cries out, "Stay out of the alleys. The cops are beating people in there."

"Stay out of the alleys; the cops are beating people in there."

At a hotel lobby, a medic begs for water. A police sergeant chases him away, brandishing a club. We walk west one block to Wabash. For the first time since the attack began, the air smells fairly clean. I recall my first contact with toxic and non-toxic gas. It came during the war when, as a recruit, I was required to enter a quonset hut in which various gasses were released before I was permitted to put my mask on. In this way I became acquainted with the smell of different gasses and proficient in placing a gas mask on quickly. As it developed, however, the training was not necessary. The Nazis did not utilize gas.

Now we are walking slowly, breathing deeply, as we pass 13th Street, going north, toward the Hilton. We reach Roosevelt and walk east toward Michigan. Just past Wabash, on Roosevelt, I see a parked, unmarked car, with two men sitting in it wearing gas masks. I ask Carolyn to take a picture of them and she does. They look up and say something, but it is unintelligible. We hurry on.

Then I stop, look back and try to note the license plate. My sight is too blurred to make it out, but the two men could not know that. They leap out of the car and shout, "Stop." We continue on. One shouts, "Stop, or I'll shoot." Carolyn suggests we ignore them. I insist that we stop.

They come running up. Both wear guns, one wields a club. "Why did you take our picture?" one demands. I am six feet, but both are taller than I. Without their masks they look like hoods, and they are hardly more intelligible than with them.

I decided not to share my thinking on this matter with them. "What's wrong with taking your picture?" I ask.

134

"O.K., wise guy, let's have that camera," one says, reaching for the camera that Carolyn is not about to surrender.

"Just wait a minute," I say. "Here are my press credentials." I do not think, on reflection, that I could have made a more serious mistake. Goering said that when he heard the word culture, he reached for his gun. I doubt that these two often had a chance to respond to that word, but "press" brought about a similar reaction. One grabbed the camera, the other reached for me.

"Would you like to see my District Attorney's credentials now?" I ask. In order to facilitate my work in New Orleans, Jim Garrison, the New Orleans District Attorney, has given me investigator's credentials. No doubt Garrison could not win a popularity poll with the Chicago cops—who could besides Daley or Wallace?—but I am counting on their inability to read quickly, or at all.

"What?" was all that one of them could manage. I take out the credentials with the words "District Attorney's Office" predominating, and he says, "O.K. Yeah, I guess it's O.K." I took this as a type of apology, and Carolyn and I left to walk east as they went back to the car. I was relieved to have escaped with the film, which I was sure we would lose, and to have escaped being slugged as well.

After we had gone about ten steps, Carolyn turns

Two camera-shy Chicago police officers in an unmarked automobile.

and shouts back to them, "And you had better watch it next time." Not to be outdone, one of them offered a bit of repartee that he had probably prepared for the occasion: "Oh, yeah."

I take Carolyn's arm and suggest that we get out of there.

We escape into the Hilton area to find that the Guard is firing cannisters of gas into the park area across the street. We pass two Guardsmen loading their pistols. Carolyn tries to get a picture, and one of them points the loaded pistol at her. I say gruffly for the first time, "Forget this one," and we move on. A jeep with a machine gun mounted on it turns onto Michigan. I hear the soft pop indicating that another gas cannister has been exploded. At the convention, Hubert Humphery is making a speech. He says that "we witnessed" a "desperate attempt of tyranny to crush out the forces of liberalism by force and brutal power, to hold back change." He is talking about Czechoslovakia.

As the gas gradually dissipates, we return to the park across the street from the hotel to await the return of the delegates. The National Guard, now without masks, is lined up in the street, standing at the east curb and facing us. A young man holds a young girl. He addresses no particular soldier as he says, "Wouldn't you rather hold a girl than a gun? Why don't you put that thing down and join us?"

A sergeant paces back and forth just behind the line of soldiers. "You can listen to them but don't talk to them," he says.

A bearded man in his late twenties walks up to a soldier. He is well dressed and speaks with a very soft

137

voice. His manner is confidential as he leans toward a young soldier and asks, "Do you have any grass?" There is no reply. "Oh, come on, I know you fellows all smoke on occasion."

The sergeant walks over, again warns the men not to talk, then marches away. "I'll bet the sergeant has some, right?" Several soldiers smile. Encouraged by the response, he continues, "You fellows probably don't have a radio so I should give you the latest news. Hubert Nixon has just been nominated here in Miami. He will take on Richard Humphrey. Who are you going to vote for? I mean it. Really, is there any choice this year? That's why we're here, you know. We don't like being gassed. But we would like a choice."

It is one minute to eleven. The guard is ordered to put on gas masks. The demonstrators remain calm. Few move. They begin to chant, "The whole world is watching. The whole world is watching." In the park, the singing starts again. From the last, well-guarded bull horn, comes a voice. "They will not toss that gas while we're singing. No one is that inhuman. Not the guard, not the pigs, no one." The singing begins:

"Oh, say can you see
by the dawn's early light . . ."

In the park, we stand and sing. The soldiers are perplexed. No order to stand at attention has been given.

Yet it's the National Anthem. But they have been ordered to ignore us. A number come to attention, some remove masks, some stand at ease. In the Hilton, some windows open up. The gas is still swirling around up there, so the windows open just a bit. The words of the song and the gas enter the rooms together, borne by the same breeze from Lake Michigan. At eleven fifteen the gas masks are removed. The curfew will be relaxed another night, it seems.

I walk to Balbo and Michigan. A boy is sitting in the street writing on the white paint that divides east and west traffic. He writes, "Peace Now," and draws a rather crude dove.

We sit on the grass and sing. The guard seems spent. The energy for another charge seems to be lacking. It is now 1:15. A Bishop of the Episcopal Church arrives. His name is Bishop Edward Crowther. He says he was in California and he saw "those incredible scenes on television." He says, "And so I came here at once for holy communion. We are the reconcilers. We belong here. I came here to express my concern and to offer my services." He points into the park and says, "I understand that the first cannister of gas exploded by the cross over there. That is appropriate."

139

# the raid on the hilton

I managed about three hours sleep in the south-side motel late that Friday morning. As dawn broke, the police, not the demonstrators, raided the Hilton. They invaded the rooms occupied by Senator McCarthy's campaign organization on the hotel's fifteenth floor. They dragged campaign workers from their beds and forced them to go to the main lobby. John Warren, a twenty-four year old graduate of the University of Chicago Law School and McCarthy's campaign co-ordinator for Arkansas, was beaten over the head with a night stick. His head was cut open. Dr. William Davidson, a Boston physician and chief medical aide for the McCarthy headquarters, treated three of the wounded and then sent them to Michael Reese Hospital. McCarthy's neice, Beth McCarthy, was forced by the police to leave her room.

Two young workers suffered serious head cuts; one

required ten stiches, another six stitches. Others were bruised.

McCarthy rushed to the lobby to comfort his staff workers, who had been forced to remain there by the police. He said, "I am shocked beyond belief."

The Police Department explained that the officers' behavior was motivated by two factors. The rooms were supposed to have been vacant, the Department claimed. The police also said that objects, including smoked fish, had been thrown from the windows. It would have been extremely difficult to fix, with any degree of certainty, the exact origin of an object thrown from the hotel. This would be particularly true of an object allegedly hurled from an upper floor. The occupants of the rooms denied throwing anything out of the windows. A subsequent trial might have disclosed the basis for police action, but the police, in what hardly may be described as a show of confidence in their evidence, declined to arrest anyone.

The question as to the legitimacy of the occupation of the rooms by the McCarthy staffers may be determined beyond dispute.

However, to my knowledge, no reporter looked into and wrote about that aspect of the dispute..

I arrived at the Conrad Hilton early that afternoon and asked to speak with the assistant manager, who was on duty in the lobby. The red plush carpeting reeked with the smell of vomit, making me anxious to complete the mission as soon as possible. I told the assistant manager that I had stopped at the Conrad Hilton on several occasions, that I had patronized other Hilton establishments, and that I held a Carte Blanche card. I told him also that I stood ready to sacrifice these advantages of life in an abundant society if I was not given information about the shameful events that had taken place there some hours before. He suggested that I talk with the "publicity and advertising department" on the fourth floor. Instead I called upon Dick Kampert, the Director of Security for the hotel.

I introduced myself and said that I wanted to know why the young people were evicted from the McCarthy rooms. He asked what my interest was. I explained that I might wish to write about it, and that in any event, I would have a rather uneasy feeling about ever staying in a Hilton hotel in the future if I thought that the security forces, there to protect me, might instead invite the local police in to evict me. "Oh, we didn't invite them, they just came in on their own," was his reply.

*Lane*: Well, now we're getting somewhere. Why did you let them in?

*Kampert*: Well, they were throwing things out of the window.

*Lane*: Did you see them do that yourself?

*Kampert*: No, I heard about it later on television.

*Lane*: I see. Now again, why did you allow the cops to enter and evict your guests?

*Kampert*: Well, I mean, how can you stop the cops?

*Lane*: Were the McCarthy people your guests?

*Kampert*: What do you mean?

*Lane*: You know what I mean. Was the room rented to them or was it supposed to be vacant?

*Kampert*: I don't know.

*Lane*: That's not true. This is the only damn hotel in the world with an IBM card for every guest and every room.

*Kampert*: Well, we are looking into that now. We haven't completed our investigation.

*Lane*: I don't care about your completed investigation. You can check that IBM card and know in ten seconds whether the room was supposed to be occupied or vacant. I cannot believe that you are so negligent not to have done that yet. They were evicted hours ago.

*Kampert*: O. K.

*Lane*: What does that mean?

*Kampert*: Yes, it was occupied.

*Lane*: I know it was occupied. Was it supposed to have been occupied?

*Kampert*: Yes.

*Lane*: By the McCarthy people? By the people the cops dragged out?

*Kampert*: Yes.

*Lane*: Then how could you let the police into a room to evict a registered guest?

*Kampert*: I can't control the police.

*Lane*: Did you try to stop them?

*Kampert*: No.

On Thursday, Daley had defended the police department's actions at a press conference. The *Chicago Tribune,* his most ardent supporter, said, "After reading a statement in a press conference, Daley abruptly left without answering questions." As proof that the demonstrators were "terrorists," Daley said that they had come to Chicago "with helmets and with their own brigade of medics." Some even had "maps locating the hotels," he charged. Despite findings of such substance, criticism of the police continued, both in America and in Europe. As the young people had hoped, the whole world was indeed watching.

When the unprecedented dawn attack upon the offices of Sen. McCarthy brought a new wave of critical comment, Daley came forward with another story. As he put it himself, "This is something I have never said to anyone." His disclosure; "There were reports and intelligence on my desk that certain people planned to assassinate the three contenders for the Presidency, many of the leaders, including myself, but I've had that constantly." He refused to say who the "certain people" were. The three men who were to have been murdered—Humphrey, McCarthy and McGovern.

The story was given banner headline treatment in Chicago, practically driving everything else off front pages. It dwarfed the coverage given to the raid on the McCarthy quarters. As Daley probably calculated it would, it brought about a change in attitude of many people, who began to reason that Daley, faced with such awful prospects, was forced to take action.

Never mind that such reasoning was specious; the entirely unsupported announcement had accomplished its purpose. Not many hours before, McCarthy had brushed aside his Secret Service protection and walked into the park to address the demonstrators. He was unprotected. Why had Daley "never said anything" to McCarthy, if his life was in danger? Why had McCarthy not been struck down, but wildly cheered instead, when he spoke, unprotected, to thousands of the demonstrators, if he was, as the Mayor stated, on their target list? Why had the "certain people" not been apprehended and charged with conspiracy to commit murder, and thus removed as a threat to the lives of the leaders? Since Daley had previously reported that he was working closely with the United States Department of Justice, why had he failed to share his intelligence with that agency? Attorney-General Ramsey Clark appeared to be unaware of the validity of Daley's secret reports and intelligence when he spoke two and one half weeks later. Indeed Clark was highly critical of the Chicago police effort. He said that police action "in excess of authority" is the most dangerous of all types of violence "because it leaves the public without protection." He condemned "excessive force and violence by police." He said that the "clear offer of a fair and reasonable accommodation of requests to assemble and speak reduces the risk of violence." The press reported that Clark "left little doubt that he was speaking of the activities of Mayor Daley and his police force." And he added, apparently in direct answer to Daley's much heralded assassination conspiracy: "Careful sifting of rumors can eliminate the ninety-nine percent that are obviously unfounded, without escalating public apprehension by giving them credibility."

If there had been a plan afoot to kill the contenders, Daley and his police force acted in such a fashion as to increase the likelihood of its success. Instead of arresting the culprits, the police rioted, thus creating the very disorder that could assist a hidden assassin. But logic, as Daley knows so well, plays no part in the making of a headline. He had released his highly dubious bombshell and it had found its target.

The unnamed certain people could not even demand equal time. The police have a phrase for this. In their language, Daley, like his cops before him, had taken a cheap shot.

# CHAPTER X

# reflections

Chicago did not seem real while I was there. Now, far away from that city, nothing else does.

I have retreated to Denmark to think about what I witnessed, and to write. I write in a peaceful cabin just above the Baltic Sea. This place was once a refuge for me, but now it provides no comfort. Relieved as I was to leave Chicago, I am now anxious to return. I can no more articulate the reasons than could that youngster on the street when he was asked why he stayed.

I read a note that I wrote to myself in my Thursday, August 29th, notebook.

"Humphrey's approval of the police, refusal to condemn Daley, will encourage cops in Chi and everywhere. Brutality condoned. When Pres. candidate places seal of approval on beating unarmed kids we are no longer what we were. What are we now? NOTE—Check newspapers to see if police in other cites establish new precedents. Blacks weren't here in numbers but they may suffer the most in future police riot situations."

I never did follow through on that advice to myself clipping newspapers from throughout the country. Yet there hardly was any need to. The next day the Chicago police department announced that police officer Richard Nuccio, convicted of murder, would not be dismissed from the force, making Chicago possibly the only city to maintain a police force with a duly certified murderer on it.

A week later a group of approximately 150 white men, most of them New York City police officers, attacked a small number of Negroes on the sixth floor of a New York City Courthouse in Brooklyn. Some of the officers, swinging blackjacks, were wearing "Wallace for President" campaign buttons. The off-duty policemen wore revolvers. Several of the victims suffered head injuries, including a girl who attends Columbia University. A reporter for the *New York Post* said that he had been kicked several times as he walked about with a notebook. In a burgeoning police state accurate reportage is the enemy, the reporter the opponent, the photographer the adversary. A camera or a notebook is both an indication of hositlity and an invitation to attack.

149

We are, most assuredly, not where we once were. Not just our children, but Justice, has been alienated, as the young people were so quick to understand. The police are the instruments of the state. Their function is, to a large extent, executive. As peace officers they are obligated to enforce the law with impartiality. No reasonable man may any longer state that the police provide that service. When they fall, and when they become instruments of oppression, the public is faced with a decision. Clark states that the public is left without protection in such circumstances. Those who become victims of the police may remain without protection, or organize themselves to provide it. Thus, the entirely predictable phenomenon of the Black Panthers.

The police, by the very nature of their assignments, have another important responsibility. Police officers play a judicial role as well. In many cases, perhaps most, the testimony of the policeman is decisive. Since both the officers and the judges are instruments of the state, the testimony of the officers is generally accepted without serious reservation. Often just the slightest distortion, a minor exaggeration during direct examination, or in the making out of an affidavit accompanying a complaint, will suffice to secure a finding of guilt, even though the defendant is innocent.

More than six hundred demonstrators were arrested in Chicago. I saw many arrests effected by the police, yet not once did I witness a valid arrest. Some missiles were thrown at the police lines; but not once, in my presence, were the police able to locate the culprit. Rarely did they even bother to look, satisfying themselves by striking out at or arresting whoever was at hand.

The first act of violence was to strike an innocent man. The second, to arrest him, having embarked upon such a course of conduct. Is it not reasonable to assume that the officer, when called upon to testify and to justify his improper conduct might very well make a false statement? Whatever the motivation for his original act, his course of conduct, once begun, almost constrains him to swear falsely. If not that, then he must admit that his arrest was falsely made. And thus the delicate balance of justice, so assiduously arrived at through centuries of thought, becomes an anachronism. Justice is gone and those who understand that fact become further alienated from a society which pretends to be that which it may have once been, but no longer is. The young do not suffer hypocrisy gladly.

What is the meaning of Chicago? The campaign of Senator Eugene McCarthy began in New Hampshire with his statement that he hoped to get the young people of America off the streets and into the institutions that exist in a democratic society. Hippies and the other disinherited left their uninvolvement behind to join with him. They were with him throughout the several state campaigns. They saw the forces that represented peace victorious

151

in every contest where the people were permitted to vote and the forces that represented the old order go down to defeat. In Chicago they discovered that the institutions were no longer open, that America had become a closed society. Those who traveled to the convention could not even walk to within three miles of the convention hall, while Mayor Daley's sycophants handed out "We Love Daley" signs and false but acceptable credentials to hundreds of those on the Mayor's payroll, who were also bussed from the Mayor's own political clubhouse to reserved seats at the Amphitheatre. Thus was the voice of the people served.

Before it was all over, the children were back on the streets; but by then even the streets and parks were closed. Before it was all over, the McCarthy delegates were on the streets with them, and in the jail cells as well.

Thus had we become something that we never were before.


September, 1968
Ulslev Strand
Denmark